Lions & Tigers & Bears

by

ALICIA WILLIAMS

A Novel Published by Ècrivez!
Columbus, Ohio

This novel is a work of fiction. All names, characters, dialogues, incidents, and places are a product of the author's imagination and are not to be construed as real. This work does not depict or portay any particular gender or group of people. Any resemblance to actual events, locales, or real persons (living or dead) is entirely coincidental.

Lions & Tigers & Bears.
Copyright © 1999 by Nancy Hill-McClary

ISBN: 1-889316-02-4
Cover design by Daves' Forms Design and Gaius Griffea "Blue"
Page layout and design by Moonlighters Ink
Back cover photograph taken by Chetti
First edition published and distributed by Ècrivez!,
September 1999.

Acknowledgment

You should know that many positive, spirited people have supported me and given me the opportunity to speak, educate, laugh, and just share some good times as an author since I wrote my first book in 1996. For this effort, I particularly want to acknowledge my loving mom, Lorraine M. Hill, who travels with me, except when she takes a city bus tour; Mrs. Goins' B-1, B-2, and B-3 Reading and Language Arts classes at Monroe Alternative School in Columbus, Ohio; the Open Book Closed Chapter Reading Group; Carolyn Stokes, who is an inspiration to many; members of the National Black Police Association (NBPA); *Joy's four sisterfriends* (they know who they are), and...ya know, New Jersey's in the House!

Next, there are five individuals who read the initial draft copy of my first novel. They are: my unconditionally supportive and giving sister, Valerie M. Orr, new grandmother to my two-year-old great-nephew, Christopher Alexander Orr; Phyllis Cartwright Diehl, a true lady (I wanna be like her as our friendship continues to grow and *thicken*); Howard Grinter (Jerry, to some folk), my spiritual colleague at St. Dominic Church and buddy-L; Bea Weaver, my favorite "EOM" (that's editor-of-me) person and dearest friend for many years; and last, but not least is "EVANZ!" known to many, particularly her mama, as Sharon K. Evans (Hey Kenny!). You came thru for me on crunch time, girlfriend. I owe you much more than a CD!

Big THANKS to anyone who owns an Alicia Williams' book. I am very appreciative of your support.

And finally, to my family in Ohio, Michigan, New York, Illinois, North Carolina, Missouri, Pennsylvania, and Florida...Luv ya...enjoy No. 3! Another is forthcoming in 2000!

Dedication

I wish to dedicate this novel to

Him because He directs all of our paths,

and to give much thanks to

Him for my creativity and all the

blessings bestowed on me for

the past forty-one and a half years.

Contents

🌸
This is Alicia
...and *I have a few suggestions*

...enjoy the book as much as the reggae room.

...it is suitable for Shadowlands, okay?

...it might be better than drum world.

...it definitely beats jazzy-zoo events.

...now don't read and drive the purple car!

...you should know that lions can interpret
for aliens.

...please set the mood with the purple scents.

...L,...then M,...but N will always represent!

...*L's to U's to 2's,* T-Mgr-Dr-Mn.

ALSO BY

Alicia Williams

THE SCARECROW, THE LION & THE TINMAN:
A Novelette About Forbidden Friendships

WOMEN BEHIND THE MEN BEHIND THE BADGE:
Their Stories

prologue
(A Sequel to *The Scarecrow,*
The Lion & The Tinman)

LaNae...Stretching the Friendship Lines

LaNae Nelson had received a note from Solomon on Friday. She took a few deep breaths as she took the small envelope out of the larger interoffice mailing envelope. She recognized his neat printing and smiled fondly knowing he was again taking an opportunity to secretly communicate with her. Had Solomon referred to her as his soul mate in the note? About a year and a half ago, he apologized for taking the reassignment to work in Baltimore (only to return to his old job in Indianapolis), and for not telling her of his decision. He said he could never stop being her friend because they had some type of lifetime bond. In his most recent note he had even gotten enough courage to tell her that "yes," he would love her forever. Solomon added that he did not expect her to leave her husband for him. (Couldn't this be his way of telling LaNae that *he* had no intentions of leaving his wife?) His note had finally stated that

1

he would always be committed to her as a loving friend. He also said he hoped that she would always be his friend as well. He ended the note with "CU LU." It was simple. Straight and to the point.

As manager of the Accounts Payable Department in the Baltimore office of NTM Advertising firm, LaNae sat at her desk and read his five lines of printed text. She had already read it over twice. She began her own personal letter back to him on light blue stationery:

*You again are some piece of work. Your short note to me was **quite enjoyable**. I will have to destroy it some day, but not now. A year and a half ago, I can remember telling you when we decided to be friends that the close relationship we have is one to keep. The only difference now is that because we are friends and old familiar lovers, the capacity of what we have has no limits. We both know how far "It," "Us," this relationship, or friendship (call it what you want) etc. can go. We have spouses to keep us both in check and so our lives have become nothing more than secrets and lies.*

I made the travel arrangements for my fortieth birthday and Joy, Monique, and I are going on a western Caribbean cruise in about three months to celebrate. I thought about inviting you. They don't have to know you are on board until they happen to see you on the ship. If you decide to accept my invitation, I won't care what anyone thinks. I know Joy suspects that we are involved again but she just won't say anything. You know, it's our business and she'll have much to say. But I'm gonna do what I want with who I want and when I want. Even Joy knows that about me. Monique respects me for that kind of thinking. I'll let you know when I decide to tell them about us. I realize that this trip could provide the potential setting for me to tell them everything.

You are so very forbidden to me. I feel like I've been concealing my thoughts and feelings about you. You were right when you said what's not communicated isn't necessarily unsaid. I do understand why we call and write each other long distance. We both know how good this relationship is.

*I guess I would like to know just how far you would like us to go. Can we really continue to give to each and stay married? (I have **not** worked out any details on how to accomplish this.) Or, should we end our respective marriages and get on with our business at hand. We have a long history together and we know we love each other. I mean always and forever, just like my favorite song. I need some piece of mind and release from my impulsive desire and fantasy to be with you. I believe you need the release as well since I keep hearing and reading about how you feel about me. Part of me is ready to be with you, which makes me **dangerous**. And that's the truth.*

I keep asking myself where does your relationship with your wife and mine with my husband Freddy go when we spend such quality and quantity of time (mostly on the phone) with each other. I don't want to think we are unfaithful, although I know deep inside my heart that unfaithful is exactly what and who we are.

*Needless to say, you have given me double pleasure for being my long-time loving friend (and you know that's what bonds us) and then over the years you have been able to **show me** what type of real love a man can have for a woman, which has helped to make us soul mates as you mentioned in your note.*

I had to write you, Solomon, what can I say? I wanted to be up front with you because our doors are opened even wider now. Do you understand that for the first time in my life (our lives) I am giving some serious thought to making a change in my life that may allow me to spend time with you on a more permanent basis? I realize now that I could leave my husband and disrupt my life for you, but I won't without a serious commitment from you and knowing what sacrifices you are willing to make in your life for me.

Keeping "us" a secret has been hard. We won't be able to keep up with all of the lies we've told forever. So part of me wants you on that ship so we can test the waters, so to say, and talk in great detail about how we're going to deal with our situation. We may not admit it, but we do care what our family and friends think. The real question at hand is: Are we ready to make a commitment to be together?

*Let me know as soon as you can if you would even consider going on a cruise with me in April. Then I can decide whether to extend you a **personal** invitation.*

LU2, LaNae

LaNae placed the blue ball-point pen in the coffee mug sitting on her desk. After neatly folding the three pages in half, she inserted them in the matching blue envelope. She put the envelope inside an interoffice mailer and addressed it to: "S. E. Moore c/o NTM Indianapolis Site." Then she wrote "L. Nelson" and her room number in the upper left-hand corner. LaNae decided to make a trip down to the basement to mail processing. Placing this particularly personal letter in the "outgoing" mailbox just outside her office wouldn't be a very smart move. Her young secretary, Mary, was just a little too nosey.

Monique...All the Right Places

Monique Payne headed

to the boarding area to check in early. Her nonstop flight to Indianapolis was scheduled to leave at nine this morning from La Guardia airport. It was now seven-thirty, but this time Monique would appreciate the wait...this time and for the first time. Being the impatient person that she was, the hour plus wait would have driven her crazy. But during her short stay in New York, Monique had allowed herself to be tended to in all the right places and had also done some tending to of her own. Therefore, she had much on her mind to think about. A few *nice* thoughts and *fond memories*. Some visual images that only she could recall and reflect on, particularly with her eyes closed. When she did this it enabled her to re-live the experience once again. When she as much as thought about what had happened in that day and a half it gave her a good private feeling deep down inside.

Monique worked in Accounts Payable and Receivable at NTM Advertising firm. The company had sent her to this two-day spring conference for the Society of Minority Professionals whose members had shortened the name to "The Profs." The membership was made up of about eight hundred who lived and worked throughout the United States in many different professions, ranging from those who specialized in the legal, financial, and medical fields to the librarians and educators.

Monique had arrived in New York late Wednesday evening and had even worked that day because she had plenty of time to catch the late flight out. The conference began Thursday and ended on Friday. Her airline ticket ended up costing the company less if she stayed the weekend so she was scheduled to fly back on Sunday. She stayed at the Grand Hyatt in Manhattan where the conference was held. It was quite productive, and Monique was able to meet several people with whom she gladly exchanged business cards and shared ideas about coping in the professional arena as a minority. It was good to hang out with such positive Black men and women. True movers and shakers on this earth. Some members of The Profs had even made personal commitments to continuously recommend minority candidates for hire to personnel reps in their respective companies. Many companies are quite insensitive to the need to consistently recruit minorities, including women, into professional positions and they are even less concerned about promoting them once they are hired. Members of The Profs made it their business to bring these types of concerns to the attention of their company decision makers. Sometimes it *did* make a difference.

The minority conference always included the annual formal scholarship ball that was usually held on Friday, the last day. Proceeds from this twenty-dollar-a-ticket fund raiser went toward The Profs' freshman book fund. Monique never missed this dressy affair. She could even attend the event by herself because most of the attendees usually went to the affair so she would be among people she knew. This particular year Monique decided to wear her full length, sleeveless black and gold lamé dress. It fit her, but it was not so fitting that every shapely angle of her body was out for show. It didn't matter though because Monique had the kind of body that made her look sharp and classy no matter what outfit she wore.

She stepped into the huge ballroom on the third floor where the party was to be held and to her surprise only a few couples and about five single men had arrived. It was ten o'clock and obvious to Monique that the real party animals were waiting for the stroke of midnight to show up *and* to be seen. Monique didn't have the time or the energy for the two-hour wait. She started toward the escalator steps intending to go down one floor to the big screen TV and lounge area to order one drink before she called it a night. What a waste of a good dress, she thought.

As Monique rode the escalator down she caught a glimpse of his profile first, then a complete view of *him* sitting in one of the high back chairs watching a movie. His *very* nice eyes, seductive smile, well-trimmed thick black moustache with a hint of gray were all noticeable assets. She guessed him to be in his mid-to-late forties or early fifties. When their eyes finally met, it was mutual attraction and they both respected it by not breaking eye contact. His broad smile was an obvious indication of how comfortable he was flirting with women. She gave him her best confirming nod and added a half-smile. He sat upright as the escalator steps brought her down to his floor level.

Monique walked right past him looking off to the left toward the bar. He tried to appear cool, casually dressed in a gray and dark blue diagonal patterned short-sleeve shirt (one of those golfing types) and dark blue pants. He was wearing sandals.

Monique walked to the bar, ordered her drink, and then paid for it. She expected to sip it for just a few minutes alone. This wasn't going to take very long. She figured ten or fifteen minutes at the most and then she'd head for the elevators to go to her room. By then it would probably be about ten-thirty. As she proceeded to a cluster of chairs and a love seat in front of a small table, she didn't know whether she blinked and had somehow missed him or whether he had performed one of the best magic acts *ever* because *now* he was sitting in the love seat that she was heading precisely toward. There was no way for her to change directions and not look awkward. She *had* to walk toward him. He just sat there enjoying her attractiveness and the gracefulness of her paced walk. She had to admit she appreciated the satisfied look on his face and the way he sat with his legs crossed wearing those dark blue sandals. It wasn't just his smile. It was that confident look on his face as he stood up to pull one of the chairs back from the table for her to sit down. It was as if he *knew* Monique wouldn't walk the other way.

Well, long story short...they talked until about three in the morning. It was easy for them to talk but not so easy to stay awake into the wee hours so they agreed they both needed to get a *little* sleep before their Saturday brunch date. They slept in their own hotel rooms that night and Monique packed most of her things the next morning. He had asked if she wanted to have brunch on Saturday in his room around ten-thirty. He was going to order room service. After brunch, they took a nap in separate beds although the beds were in *his* room. When they woke up they decided to spend the day together. Their meals were ordered via room service again. Luckily, Monique had packed. She didn't leave his room until seven Sunday morning. She didn't know when he had to be packed or when his flight left. She didn't care either, she had a plane to catch at nine.

"We will start boarding in about fifteen minutes," the male flight attendant announced over the intercom. Too bad they couldn't leave for the airport together on Sunday, she thought to herself, not wanting to refocus on her present surroundings for the first time since she had sat down. Surprising to her, about thirty people had arrived to await the departure of the plane for Indianapolis. Monique continued to reminisce about the events that took place yesterday as

best she could given the crowd and their busy conversations. She really wanted to hear from him. She wasn't anxious to tell Joy and LaNae, her two best friends, about her one and a half-day "liaison." At least not now. The cruise for LaNae's birthday in April would be the right time to make her business known.

It would be more exciting if *he* could actually be on the ship, but Monique knew there was no chance of that *ever* happening. She had no way of contacting him. They had decided not to share any personal information about themselves. They were just going to *experience* each other for the day. They didn't even know what each other did for a living. They spent some quality time together and yes he did touch her both physically and emotionally and *in all the right places*. It wasn't about making love. It was better than that.

Hailey...We Play in a Feminine Way

Hailey Woods came to the conclusion that she had been playing the flirting game with men for quite some time. As Hailey poured bubble bath *and* her favorite berry scented bath oil into the water that begin to fill her oval shaped whirlpool tub, she began to think. It was six-thirty Friday night and Paul her husband had taken their son Jake to a birthday pizza party. She couldn't wait to get them out of the house so she could relax alone for once and do some soul searching about her life and the way she went about living it. Her husband and son would be gone for two hours.

The water was a little on the hot side because Hailey liked taking hot baths. She simply tossed her left foot in and out of the water quickly until her foot could tolerate the temperature enough to go in all the way. She did the same thing with the right foot before she immersed more of her legs into the water. After stooping in the water and adjusting *that* part of her body to the water's temperature, she was able to sit down completely, stretch out her legs, and lean back, allowing every inch of her body up to her neck to enter the water. She didn't want the bath water to become luke warm five minutes after she began to veg out and enjoy the comforts of her relaxing soak.

The bubbles in the tub surrounded her entire body and few had dissipated. Her very sexy body was covered with suds. The berry aroma rose, permeating the entire bathroom with a light, sweet flowery scent. Classical music played softly in the background from the stereo in her bedroom. The large mulberry-scented candle illuminated the bathroom in a delicate way, creating an atmosphere that was perfect for thinking *and fantasizing*. Hailey definitely allowed her mind to wander and her thoughts to escape freely. She was alone to ponder about her lifestyle if she desired and why she had become such a flirt and tease at age thirty-one.

"*I've had it too good,*" Hailey said. She moved the bubbles around in the water as she laid back in the tub. She thought again. *I wonder why I fantasize about ways to share good quality time with men. It's hard to watch a television or a movie theater scene involving a man and woman without having a personal reflection about whom I might want to interact with in the same way.*

She had no intentions of having a serious affair or fling again because she didn't think anyone was safe from getting AIDS. That little scare she had two years ago was a real wake up call for her Besides that...she didn't always forget that she was actully still very married.

Pondering over the question of why she had such a genuine desire to play games with men, Hailey sat upright in the tub and stroked her legs and arms slowly with a thick, cream-colored wash cloth. She had obviously put enough bath soap in her water because many of the bubbles still remained. "*I know why I play,*" she stated proudly. This time out loud as if she needed to make public amends for her actions. "*I do it for the attention,*" she said matter-of-factly. "*Men have to get their egos stroked and women have egos that need to be stroked too!*"

Hailey began to meditate on this and came to the conclusion that both men and women have bottomless cups of emotional desires and needs that they anticipate a mate will fill. This anticipation drives their search for that mate. It doesn't matter who fills the cup because it will never overflow and always needs replenishing. It remains in a state of being half empty or half full depending on one's level of emotional need and greed.

Hailey was completely relaxed now. The bubbles and berry scents allowed her to soon recall what Joy, her very good friend, had said a few years ago about finding a mate. Everyone, according to Joy, should know themselves emotionally, spiritually, sexually, and financially. If they have things "in check," as Joy had put it, they will radiate a positive energy that will attract a mate. Hailey had totally agreed with Joy because she did feel good about herself and did want to make everyone around her feel good too. Sometimes men at NTM, the advertising firm where she worked, had to be put in their places because they wanted to "tap" (in a subtle way through a daily phone call or regular office visit) some of the energy that Hailey was radiating. Others wanted to walk in her shadow and live off her energy. Hailey wasn't giving any of herself to anyone free. She was gonna get something back in return.

During her thirty-minute soak, Hailey half-heartedly played with the bubbles in a childlike manner. She thought about how much her husband should count in her life, but at the same time how rarely he was around her when she was radiating full strength. She now had to rely on quality when it came to time spent with her husband. Quantity left many years ago.

Joy had asked Hailey if she wanted to take a western Caribbean cruise with her and a few of her friends at NTM in about three months. Hailey wasn't sure if she trusted herself on a ship with potentially single men (and those *single-acting* married men). Hailey realized that she had no desire to completely stop her game playing. She smiled as she slid down into the tub making the water rise just to the top of her bare shoulders. Most of the bubbles were gone. Now Hailey washed her entire body with the gel soap that sat on the tub's counter. The water was just beginning to lower in temperature, but the berry bath oil scent still lingered full strength. *"I'm going on that cruise!"* Hailey exclaimed. *"Who knows, maybe I'll be able to get some of this game playing out of my system."* She carefully stepped out of the water and onto the small bath mat where she stood nude and dripping wet. The bath water drained from the tub as Hailey reached for the thick bath towel to dry herself.

Joy...What Motivates Men and Women in Relationships?

Joy Sharpe unlocked the small cabinet on the left side of the headboard of the king size mahogony waterbed. There was a cabinet on one side and a bookshelf for her collection of the latest Black-authored novels on the other. Both sides had built-in vanity lights. Joy and her husband Peter were avid book readers. The cabinet was always locked and Joy had the only key. Peter had no problems with Joy having the key to this cabinet and he also knew she kept her private diary in there. He wasn't interested in reading the diary either. He respected her privacy. He had his own personal diary locked in a secret panel inside the bar in their finished basement. Joy didn't know about *his* diary.

She was in the mood to write. Peter was downstairs watching TV. Some sporting event was on. She wasn't sure whether it was wrestling or football. All she knew was that at four o'clock in the afternoon every Sunday or Saturday she would have at least a couple of hours to herself.

She felt a desperate need to get all of her present thoughts down on paper. This past week at work had left her a little intrigued about how men act in relationships with women. Two of the three men she had befriended years ago were still hanging around and trying to interact with her more by calling or making random visits to her office. Well, actually they were more than just friends to her at one point in her life. They were her forbidden friends (yeah, the ones she wasn't supposed to have)...her eight-to-five companions. She had asked them to give her some space about two years ago. Before telling them that, she reminded each of them in separate private meetings that their wives would probably not appreciate the attention they had so freely given her for so many years. Richard is now fifty-three, and Bryan is forty-six.

Richard's behavior is driven by the anticipation that Joy will have a weak moment and his opportunity to sample the treats again will avail itself. Bryan has just never gotten over Joy. He loves Joy hopelessly although not enough to leave his wife, but just enough to look desperate in his attempts to be with her. If anyone were to watch him, they would see through his act because it is as clear as crystal. He is no longer the smooth player Joy fell for the first time she met him. Now he stumbles every which way.

These two men have been unable to let go of the "Joy" that is deep in their hearts. Joy wondered what it was about her or what she had done to these men—and at the same time had undone years later—that would make them have such a hard time accepting the fact that she was no longer their *woman* in any emotional or personal sense. She also wondered what motivated them to want to be so attentive to her when she no longer gave them anything in return. *What actually motivates people's behavior when it comes to male-female relationships?* Joy thought about this question.

Joy began writing a response to this question on the peach colored pages of her journal. She knew her thoughts would flow liberally from her mind and then down through her fingers which held the slender black pen. She wrote the following at the top of her diary page: *Diary Entry on September 19.* Then she wrote:

What initially motivated me to interact with men on a personal level was curiosity. And yes, it did almost kill me. I am also motivated to behave the way I do with men because I seem to be able to relate to them quite well. (Some of them can be strangers and some of them are male friends I truly came to love over the years.) I respect the possibility of being attracted to a man (and he to me) enough to develop some type of involvement, be it as a friend, professional associate, close buddy, or "forbidden friend." I am very comfortable with any man I spend my time with and with whom I develop a friendship. But there have been times when I was emotionally overwhelmed.

So again, what generally motivates behavior between men and women as they interact? It's everything! Sexual desire is first and foremost!! Security is second, and the need to be pleased and ***to please*** *is probably third. Then there's love, spirituality, and trust. These last three come when a person is truly in love with another person and is finally relaxed enough to "exhale" and give some of those things back to the person who was able to give them so easily in the first place.*

She went on to write specifically about what intrigued her the most about men she had met in her life...

People in general fascinate me, but the fact that ***some*** *men continue to be bachelors all of their lives even after they marry really makes me mad. They do whatever they have to do to satisfy their egos. Some men have no expectations that their mate should fulfill their needs; therefore, they feel they don't have to fulfill the needs of their mate.*

When a man and women marry or if a couple is in a serious monogamous relationship, aren't the two of them responsible for satisfying each other's needs, no matter what they are? I am SO TIRED of men (and women too!) in relationships messin' up their lives, wasting each other's time, spinning their wheels, disrespecting each other, and not having a vision, much less an executable plan, to make their relationship of choice the best it can be. The best God has blessed it to be!

Her thoughts changed again and she decided to write just a few lines about how she felt about her best friends, all of whom were women. She had relieved some energy and felt much calmer now. She wrote:

I can honestly say that I am blessed with knowing four women who are real individuals, not fake or phony like some of the men I've met. They have positive thoughts and dreams, and are very down to earth. I have special feelings for them because they count in my life.

She was, of course, referring to her girlfriends LaNae, Monique, Shellie, and lastly, that wild and unpredictable Hailey. She, Monique, and LaNae had planned to go on a cruise in April that LaNae had been planning for two years to celebrate her upcoming fortieth birthday. Now the trip was only three months away. Joy didn't think that her two best friends would mind it she invited Shellie and Hailey to come along. She expected to hear a positive response from her two White girlfriends. She wanted to be together with all four of her sisterfriends for the first time in her life and theirs. Years ago, she had a dream that they were together in Oz. She and Monique wanted to leave Oz, Shellie and LaNae had to struggle to leave, and that Hailey had no intentions of leaving. Each of them had a scarecrow, a lion, and a tinman *male friend* who had them trapped in Oz. A weird dream, but it had many hidden subtle truths. She always thought so when it came to mind.

Joy placed the pen and diary in the headboard cabinet and locked it as she always did. Relaxed and free spirited again, she headed downstairs to sit with her husband for the last fifteen minutes of the game...or the fight...whatever was on the television. Fifteen minutes was just about all she could handle when it came to sports.

Shellie...A Left Turn in Life

Shellie Jackson had

too many thoughts running through her mind at age thirty-nine. Yet she tried to enjoy a cup of orange mango tea in her kitchen just before the sun began to rise Saturday morning around six forty-five. It's his physical presence that I will miss, not the intimacy because that began to erode many years ago. Signs of a typical warm day in Indianapolis were apparent even this early in the morning. The city would again be blessed with late summer weather temperatures in mid-September before the fall actually arrived.

Yes...it would be his physical presence that she would have to do without. She was alone and needed the time to think about so much that had happened in her life as a married woman. She needed the time to consider whether she wanted to stay married or divorce her husband of seventeen years. Surely no one expected her to make an honest commitment to STAY when so much had happened to give her so many reasons to LEAVE. But could she and her children really make it without him? She knew the answer to this question. It would be hard, but she would be okay. Nevertheless, she simply couldn't say at this hour in the morning that she wanted to leave her husband in spite of the circumstances of his affair. In all actuality, she changed her mind to leave or stay quite often. She didn't really know what she wanted to do.

She just felt sad about the whole thing. It was just another unfortunate occurrence in their marriage in which they had hurt each other again in an unforgiveable way. Another familiar road she just didn't want to go down. A road that was littered with that old familiar grief and emotional pain. Yes...those were the key words that described the last seven years of her married life with her husband Roy— emotional and painful.

Why did her relationship have so much recurring ups and downs. They both usually got through most of their problems. Shellie thought on this before taking another sip of tea. She watched the sun from her bay window as it peaked out in the distance. It wasn't too dark outside. It would soon be morning and she looked forward to the warmth of the sun's rays that usually shined brightly across her kitchen table. She had to wait. The sun was going to rise on its own accord.

I know I depend on Roy too much, Shellie thought. Roy was a willing partner in spite of the fact that he was raised in a family where nurturing and support did not exist. But it soon became obvious during *her* affair with Jeff two years ago, that perhaps Roy was not giving her enough love. Jeff, on the other hand, gave her what she needed and he did a pretty darn good job. That's probably why her affair with him lasted long enough for her to became both dependent and addicted to him. There were times when her heart ached for a phone call from Jeff. For that reason alone, she would never again rely on another man for her emotional stability.

Shellie tried to analyze her personal life. She got up to pour herself another cup of tea. The sun was starting to come up and soon her yellow kitchen walls would almost glow with the help of the sun's radiant beams. Her tea was deliciously sweetened with honey and it went down good, soothing her stomach and her wounded heart. Still she had to look at the facts and assess why she was giving some serious thought to making that left hand turn and taking her children along with her. Thus allowing her husband to continue with his life with a new partner.

She should have been able to handle his affair. After all, she was used to that type of activity. She *had* walked in those shoes for about three years. She should have been tuned into the signs of something not being right. But she wasn't. Roy never did relate to her sexually during the latter years of their marriage. He never did really turn her on either.

It's a little late now anyway and should it really matter? She felt that she deserved to be holding the bad card this time. You know you do reap what you sow, but she just wasn't ready for this. Is anyone really prepared to deal with anyone's extramarital affair? Marriage is supposed to be a sacred thing. That's a joke. You invest your heart in someone and you expect to be able to relax and enjoy the security of that investment. But maybe not. She had a lover and she could accept making that mistake. But when it came to Roy she gave him the benefit of the doubt. Who would have guessed he would have his own. A lover he had in his life even before she had met her own lover. And who would have guessed *his* lover would go by the name of Robin. Yeah...the same name as that comedian Robin Williams. The same gender too. She thought the name was kind of ironic when she considered how funny Robin Williams really was when he acted like he was gay.

Shellie hadn't told anyone about her husband being gay. Not even Joy, her very best friend. She was too embarrased. She knew Joy would be understanding, but she just couldn't come to grips with it herself. It wasn't just the affair. It was more about not being good enough to satisfy her husband to the point that he had to turn to a man to fill in the emotional gaps. Roy had decided to end his affair when she found out about it, but that was a small act of redemption.

Well Joy asked her if she wanted to take a cruise to Mexico with her two girlfriends. She didn't give her an answer because she wasn't sure if the timing was good for her to leave home right now. On the other hand, she thought that maybe the time away would be good for her mental state. Surely, she could use a little wind blowing in her hair and a couple of days out in the sun. Maybe she ought to think a little more seriously about the idea of taking this cruise with Joy. She really did need to start thinking about her own feelings for a change. She could use the time to figure out what she really wanted to do and whether her marriage still made any sense to her. Wouldn't a seven-day cruise give her an opportunity to relax her mind and her body?

Shellie decided to call Joy and tell that she wanted to be included in the upcoming festivities. The cruise was scheduled for April. After the cruise she could decide which direction she wanted to go. It could be straight ahead and she'd have to try harder to make her home life what it should be or she could make an immediate left turn and chart out a new path as a divorcee with two teenaged children.

One
The Airport Scene

It was early Sunday morning. Joy checked the two pieces of luggage she packed last night at the Delta ticket counter in the Indianapolis airport. She and her husband Peter were walking to the boarding gate for her flight, after successfully passing through the security check point. They had arrived at the airport purposely an hour and a half earlier than her seven o'clock morning flight. Peter said that he had no intentions of leaving the airport until Joy's plane departed. Joy's flight itinerary included a stop in Cincinnati, Ohio, where she had to change planes for Delta's nonstop flight to New Orleans.

Joy hoped that Monique, Hailey, and Shellie, who were also flying with her, were on route to the airport. She wanted to be there before they arrived. LaNae would also be flying to Cincinnati via an early morning Delta flight out of Baltimore where she lived. Then the five women would all fly together, as Joy had planned, to New Orleans, where their cruise ship was docked. The ship was scheduled to depart Sunday afternoon at four o'clock. The seven-day cruise had two ports of call George Town, Grand Cayman, and Playa del Carmen/Cozumel/Cancun, Mexico. The ship was sailing back to New Orleans, arriving early morning the following Sunday. Afternoon flights would bring the women back to Indianapolis and Baltimore that same day. If time permitted, they planned to visit the French Quarter in New Orleans either before or after the cruise.

"This is a public service announcement. Please keep your belongings in your possession at all times. Any belongings left unattended WILL BE confiscated. Thank you," the female voice aired over the airport intercom system.

"Why would anyone be so stupid to leave their luggage alone?" Joy said with a little hint of superiority.

"I don't know why, Joy...but people get careless and they don't watch who's watching them," Peter said in an attempt to make a subtle point to his wife that people are genuinely nonchalant and unobservant of their surroundings.

"Well the airport is just too public. You can't be too careless under these circumstances. Otherwise, you'll get your belongings taken from you," Joy said as they continued to walk toward their boarding gate.

"You have a good point, babe. We'll just make sure your stuff...I mean *our* stuff doesn't get taken because you know I'm the observant type. I don't trust anybody," Peter added, being in full agreement with his wife.

"Peter, I think sometimes you're a little too observant."

"Oh?"

"Yeah, you make me feel like everybody...I mean *every man* is out to take me away from you or something."

"Well, Joy, every man might want to try if they didn't get put in their place. I make a statement that's clear and no nonsense. I don't have any time for any game playing with the brothas or these new wave, 'wanna-kick-it-with-a-Black sista,' White guys."

"I know you don't, Peter, but I think you can relax a little. If nothing else, try smiling sometimes."

Joy's husband had sensitive caring eyes and a gorgeous smile that he seldom fully displayed in public. Around his family or hers he was not only relaxed but he loved to joke with everyone. With strangers and in unfamiliar or new surroundings, Peter purposely wore his *"do I know you?"* facial expression. It was all in the way he positioned his eyebrows and lips. The look wasn't mean or unpleasant. Most women naturally smile at him because he is quite handsome, mainly because of the conservative look he maintains. You know how some men look good in a suit and tie, and for others, it's the casual look that makes them most appealing? Well, Peter looks stunningly handsome in just about anything he wears. His clothes drape off every inch of his six foot four frame in a rather sexy way. The broadness of his chest, thickness of his arms, flatness of his stomach, curve of his waist, and shape of his buttocks...well the reality of just looking isn't satisfying enough...you really wanna "touch that body, touch that body." Usually, if a man walks past Peter he will nod with a slight smile, acknowledging Peter for having it all together. Men who are either jealous of Peter or just plain conceited will eyeball him with no smile on their face. Peter would say they were just "ego trippin'" all by themselves.

This morning Peter was clad in a cream long sleeve, short collar linen shirt worn outside over matching colored dress slacks with front tucks and bottom cuffs. He also wore bone-colored loafers.

"I am smiling Joy," Peter said. "You give me much to smile about these days."

"Oh...do I?" she said shyly, knowing that he loved her very much and that she loved him.

"Yes, we have *history* between us. I've loved you for the past seventeen years."

"I wish you could relax on that love, Peter, and not be so insecure about us."

"I wouldn't say I was insecure about our relationship, Joy. Maybe a little cautious because so many people out there want to upset happy homes simply because they are discontented with their own sad situations."

"Huh? A *little* cautious? I'm not so sure about that, Peter. You distrust people in general...sometimes a little more than they deserve to be distrusted."

"You can't always give people the benefit of the doubt, Joy. People have their own agendas, which are usually not in your or my best interest. I have a problem when someone tells me I need to be a little more trusting than I really care to be."

"I'm not suggesting that you *trust* anyone necessarily."

"Then what are you trying to say? That I should count on people to do the right thing when it comes to sampling someone else's pie?"

"No. But you probably don't have to believe that everybody wants a slice of it."

"Why not? If I were to leave MY pie sitting out, and unattended, you mean to tell me you don't think some hungry man would take a second look?"

"Probably so, Peter...but I just want you to relax and be happy and more positive about the foundation of our relationship. You make judgments about me when you make statements that suggest another man could persuade me to walk out on our marriage."

She chose her words carefully because years ago she had allowed three special male friends to get very close to her emotionally, but not enough that she considered leaving Peter to be with any one of them. Fortunately, Joy had managed to regain control of her feelings for these men and finally about two years ago she ended her involvement with all three. She was both happy and sad to have them out of her life. Happy because she no longer had to lie to herself about being Peter's faithful wife. And sad because she had developed good loving friendships with these men, and she knew they could no longer be her friends. She was reluctant to give them up, too.

"I'm comfortable with the stability of our marriage, Joy. I just want it to remain stable and I believe I have to keep my eyes open and my mind sharp. There are people out there who make it their business to start drama in other people's relationship, especially if they think by planting their drama seed something will grow just enough to raise the jealous eyebrows of one or both mates. All these home breakers want is their own personal greedy desires for someone else's mate satisfied. You can't really blame them if they feel trapped in their own relationships?"

"No, I guess not. You do have a point, Peter. But it will take more than an outside person to break us up. You know that, don't you?"

"Yeah, babe. I know. But a man's gotta do what a man's gotta do...and I'm going to protect what's mine."

"I know hon. And I would sure appreciate one of your protective hugs, right now." They stopped walking and stood facing each other. They had reached Joy's departure gate and only a few passengers had arrived that early in the morning. It was about five-forty. Joy and Peter never did mind showing their affection for each other in public. In fact, Joy often got more out of a kiss or hug when people—no more than four or five—were around to watch. He placed both hands on either side of the curves of her waist and gently squeezed her body with his finger-tips. He then kissed her lightly on the lips. Then appearing to kiss her on the cheek as well, he instead sucked the side of her cheek with his open mouth in his usual sensual way that sent orgasmic waves through Joy's whole body, starting at her neck and moving downward to her mid-section.

"Oh Peter!" Joy said before she closed her eyes to fully appreciate the brief erotic moment. It only took Peter a few seconds to perform this simple act of affection that his wife enjoyed immensely. Joy, on the other hand, would be feeling the accompanying sensations for a while longer. She hoped it would last until her plane touched down in Cincinnati.

Neither Peter nor Joy, so caught up in their moment, knew how intently a strange man, who sat in an area two clusters of seats across from where they were standing, focused his eyes on Joy. He was so hypnotized by her beauty that he could do nothing but stare at her. He was quite secluded from the few passengers who were also waiting to board. Peter, in all of cautiousness regarding Joy and men on the prowl, would have no way of knowing this stranger, who purposely wore sunglasses, was doing a more than adequate job of checking out his wife. The strange man hoped Joy was flying solo. He didn't want to have to deal with the man who accompanied her. He was obviously her husband, and he didn't want any hassles.

Peter and Joy sat down in one of the four-seater benches. They held each other's hand.

"I sure hope Hailey isn't planning to be late. I know Shellie will be on time. And Monique will probably have an attitude because our flight is so early. I really can't wait to see them all. We are going to have such a good time!" Joy said with excitement.

"I know babe. You deserve to spend time with your friends. You're gonna have a good time in New Orleans."

"I know we will. I kinda wish you were going...but then it wouldn't be an all-girl thang, now would it?"

"I guess not. But just what am I supposed to do while you're gone? Don't expect me to keep the house clean, cause I'm not picking up. I'm going to miss you too much and I won't be in the mood. I probably won't sleep good until you come back."

"You poor baby. You'll be all right. Try not to trash the house okay? You can hang out with your brother. I'm sure he'll have a few "bachelor-boy" activities lined up for the both of you. Just don't forget your present status and the fact that I own all the parts of that delicious-looking body. You do whatever you want while I'm gone, Peter, just don't hurt me. You know what I mean?"

"Yes, Joy. I would never do anything to hurt you. I love you. I know exactly what you mean," Peter was looking directly into his wife's eyes.

"I know you do, Peter. I don't want to ever hurt you either." She had rationalized quite well that what a man didn't know couldn't hurt him. And so the male companions she had in her life years ago were...well...her business and, besides that, they would remain a part of her past not her present.

"Hey, girlfriend!" Hailey bellowed out as she approached the boarding gate area where Joy and Peter were seated. Joy looked away from Peter as Hailey, dressed in the tightest size six stone-washed, light-blue jeans her body could fit, walked toward them. Hailey was glowing with excitement about their upcoming trip. She wore a low cut, long sleeve tangerine sweater (also very fitting) that just met the top of her beltless jeans, thus revealing the bare skin of her midsection in a sensuous manner. Hailey's matching tangerine colored high heel open toe sandals gave her the tall and slender look of a model.

With hair drawn up on top of her head (a few strands dangling down over her face), Hailey looked at Joy and Peter over the top rim of her small oval shaped sunglasses.

"Well, you two LOOK like you're still in love! Are you?" Hailey bellowed with a broad smile.

"Of course we are, girl! Give me a hug, Hailey! You look fabulous!" Joy screamed. She always admired her close friend. She dressed so leisurely, yet stylish, that most people, mainly men, couldn't help but take a second look at her shapely body no matter what she wore. Hailey was cute and she knew it.

"Is anyone else here yet?" Hailey asked looking at all the empty seats in the boarding gate area.

"No, not yet. I didn't expect you to be here this early. But I did expect you to be wearing something that would leave nothing to a man's imagination. You are definitely wearing those jeans *and* that top."

"Oh...you know me Joy. Just a big tease with nothing to back it up with."

"I think your body backs it up all too well. Isn't that right, hon?" Joy said looking at Peter for a quick response.

"Yeah...that's quite an outfit, Hailey," Peter said with a touch of humor in his voice. He always did feel like Hailey was a bit of a show off, but his wife's love and friendship for her made him not take her mannerisms too seriously.

"You think so, Peter?" Hailey asked. "Well you should know with a wife who wears the heck out of her own clothes, if you don't mind me speaking the truth."

Peter did know. Joy took very good care of her body and was always conscious of her weight. She was also very selective when she shopped for her clothes and his. Today she wore a yellow wraparound dress that hugged her waist and hips just the way Peter appreciated. He was a bit uncomfortable with the fact that other men would be appreciating the view as well. Joy's dress stopped several inches above her knees, which directed most eyes to her long bare shapely legs. Joy's matching yellow canvass slip-ons gave her an extra inch and a half in height.

"Now don't you two start talking about me," Joy said nudging Peter with her right elbow. Peter continued to look at his wife in an admiring way.

"Your husband knows he's got a beautiful wife...and you know he's too handsome to give up either," Hailey said smiling at her good friend and appreciating the relationship she had with her husband. She wished her own marriage was blessed with a little of whatever held Joy's and Peter's together so nicely. It wasn't that Hailey didn't love her husband, but their marriage in its seventh year had just gotten a little slow and sluggish. Neither she nor her husband put forth the effort necessary to make it what it could or should be. They avoided the issue of them,

them, instead focusing on their child who was five. Sure they were intimate from time to time, but it didn't have the same fire it once had. They loved each other but they only expressed it through the child they had created together. They were proud parents and wanted no one else to have a role in raising their son. Their relationship was one that revolved around their child. Hailey wondered what they would do if they didn't have Jake, and what Joy and Peter (who had no children) had that kept them so much in love. She promised herself that she would talk to Joy about this very topic at one point during their cruise.

The stranger looked up as Hailey, a slim White woman, joined Joy and Peter. He really liked the way Joy smiled as her friend approached her. He thought Hailey was pretty but that she lacked the sensual aurora that Joy exhibited. They were obviously pretty close friends judging by the length of their hug.

As Joy urged Hailey to sit next to her, and then re-crossed her slender legs, the stranger watched. It was easy to do from where he was sitting.

"How many pieces of luggage did you bring, Hailey?" Joy asked.

"Just two large pieces, but they roll, girlfriend. I might have to find someone really cute to help me get them on the ship."

"It's nice to know that you will never change your ways, Hailey," Joy said smiling at her friend fondly.

"Oh, Joy...will we be staying in New Orleans for a few hours before we board? I wanted to walk in the French Quarter."

"Girl, can we get to Cincinnati first?"

"Just planning ahead, girl. Just planning ahead."

"I'll bet you are. You know when we get to Cincinnati, my other friend, LaNae, who lives in Baltimore, will be arriving at the same time. Then we'll all fly in to New Orleans. Oh, in answer to your earlier question, I'm not sure how much time we'll have in New Orleans before we board the ship, Hailey. Your trip to the French Quarter may be after our cruise, depending on what time we get back to the port. Will you be okay with that?"

"Yes, but I think we'll have some time to shop or in my case 'shop look'," Hailey said. "You know I didn't have time to budget for this trip. But I'm excited about traveling with you and your friends. Thank you for asking me to go, Joy."

"Now Hailey, it wouldn't be as much fun without your wild self on that ship."

"I knew I wanted to take this trip the instant you asked me. I needed to go and Paul obviously thought the time apart would be good for us. It might be just enough of a break away for me to miss him," Hailey said contemplating her marriage situation.

"What's going on with you, two?" Joy asked out of genuine concern for Hailey. She knew Peter was listening. Knowing Hailey wouldn't want him to hear too many details, she said, "We'll talk later, okay?" Joy had openly shared many things about her own marriage with Hailey.

Changing the subject, Joy said, "Now where is the rest of our party for this cruise? I know Ms. Monique should be here by now. And Shellie...I hope her kids didn't wear her out last night. She is so attached to them. A good mother she is...but I think her kids are a little spoiled by all the attention she gives them," Joy rambled on as Hailey stood up to see if either of the two women were heading toward their gate.

Monique checked two pieces of luggage, one large trunk on rolling wheels and a tightly packed clothes carrier. She almost had to pay extra for her third piece, but it met the size requirement to carry on board the plane.

"I think I see Monique, Joy!" Hailey shouted.

As Monique approached the boarding gate area, she was not smiling. She was wearing a short sleeve ankle length dark blue stretch knit dress with a long slit on the left and gold rimmed sunglasses. The long gold chain necklace that hung from her neck matched her earrings. Wearing a pair of low heeled dark blue slip-ons, Monique walked slowly toward the three like she was the someone all were waiting to finally arrive.

"It's too early in the morning for all this drama, Joy," Monique said bluntly with her head cocked to the side. She had stopped walking and stood posing about two feet away from everyone.

"You could have kept your butt at home, girl. I'm not going to let you spoil the mood for this cruise, Monique. So stop trippin', okay?" Joy said in half serious tone.

"Just KIDDING!" Monique cried out. "I'm TOO ready to get out of this city and get on with the cruisin, drinkin, and...well...whatever you like," Monique said, now smiling and seeming to be completely relaxed. She and Joy gave each other a very tight hug.

"Hey there Hailey! How are you? You're looking *hot* as ever," Monique said as she gave Hailey a quick hug as well.

"Fine, Monique. Joy was just talking about you."

"I know she had something smart to say."

"No, not really. She was just anxious for everyone to be here...on time that is," Hailey said, looking at her watch. It was now just a few minutes to six in the morning.

"I guess since we didn't get here before Ms. Joy arrived, we're all late," Hailey said jokingly.

"Just what time did you get here, Joy? About four in the morning?" Monique asked, trying to aggravate Joy a little.

"No, Monique. I woke up at quarter to four so I could get here by five-thirty," Joy said responding truthfully to Monique's inquiry, but in joking manner.

"You were here at five-thirty this morning? Now I know you've lost your mind, Joy," Monique said.

"Monique, our flight is at seven. I believe you're supposed to check in at least one or two hours before your actual flight time. Boarding starts about fifteen or twenty minutes before the scheduled take off time so that would be about six-forty. And...giving myself an hour or two means about five-forty, right?" Joy said, explaining as much with her hands as with her mouth.

"Well Joy...you did what you obviously thought was best for you. You see I managed to get here before six...and by the way I did THAT for you. I don't want to wait too long in this airport before we take off. But let's drop it....How's you quiet husband mate over there?" Monique said looking at Peter and waiting for his response.

"I'm fine Monique," Peter said. "How are things with you and yours?" He stood up and made a gesture to shake Monique's hand.

"Everyone is fine, Peter. Thank you for asking," Monique said, ignoring his extended hand and instead giving him a more appropriate friendly hug.

"I know you're taking good care of my girl because she still looks sexy, hot, and happy! And that dress you're wearing is sharp, Joy," Monique said while taking the strap of her small carry-on bag off her shoulder to sit directly across from Joy and Peter.

"Thank you, Monique. I am pretty happy. You look good yourself," Joy said.

"I bought this dress yesterday because I like the way the material feels against my body."

"I just bet you do, Monique. What about the way it looks on you?" Joy said proud to have had Monique as a friend for over ten years.

"It's hot, huh?" Monique said, acknowledging her own good taste in clothes.

"It's you, Monique. Seductive and enticing."

"Oh well, I guess I got it that way."

"That, you do," Joy said.

The stranger wondered how Joy—so beautiful—could have yet another attractive friend, but he thought this new woman also lacked what he found mesmerizing about Joy. He assumed that they would all be flying together for one of those all-girl vacations. Did he overhear one of her friends call her "Joyce" or was it "Joy?" Either name fit her, he thought.

Hailey, Monique, and Joy continued to talk hurriedly and excitedly about the trip. It was now six o'clock and no announcements had been made about when they would be boarding the plane. In fact, an airport employee had just arrived at the gate and a lot more people were waiting in the area. Joy was a little concerned because Shellie hadn't arrived. She wondered, only for a second, whether Shellie had changed her mind and decided not to go. Joy quickly put that thought aside because it would only bring her spirits down. She wanted all four of her friends on the cruise ship with her. She couldn't bare to think about any one of them disappointing her. The bond she had with each one of these women was a tight one and she could depend on them unconditionally. They had shared many secrets (and unfortunately, a few lies).

LaNae, Monique, and Joy had established a very close friendship. These three women were like sisters to each other, so they had agreed to room together in a cabin suite on the ship. This particular cruise line reduced its cabin rate for the third adult rooming with two other passengers.

Joy also had a bonding frienship with both Shellie and Hailey, who worked in accounting at NTM. They, on the other hand, were not close friends, so they had separate cabin rooms.

Each of the four women cherished the loving friendship they had with Joy. She felt the same way about them too. This was one of the reasons each had decided to take this trip when she asked.

Roy Jackson drove up the ramp for departing flights to drop his wife off outside the terminal. Shellie had asked her husband to spare her an emotional farewell scene inside the airport. Roy was not thrilled about the fact that his wife had decided to take a cruise with some women friends at the last minute. Likewise, her two teenaged daughters didn't understand why their mother wanted to take a vacation without the whole family. Nevertheless, Shellie had no intentions of changing her plans, and she really looked forward to the time alone with "me, myself, and I" as she succinctly put it.

After checking her luggage at the ticket counter, Shellie, with a small carry-on bag, headed for her boarding gate. It was now five minutes after six.

Joy stood up to look out for Shellie. She had been waiting patiently and was only half listening to Hailey who was talking about what she was going to do in New Orleans, once again.

"I think I see Shellie coming now," Joy said to Monique and Hailey. Several people were walking toward their gate. Joy paid special attention to certain individuals in the airport. A middle-aged Black woman. A man and his wife with two small children in a two-seater baby stroller. Two airplane pilots strolling leisurely while eating a sandwich. A man in a business suit talking excitedly on his cellular phone. A flight attendant pushing an elderly White man in a wheelchair. And just behind three teenagers, Joy could see a single woman walking in a moderate pace carrying her purse and a small bag.

As Shellie got closer to the boarding gate for her flight, she thought she could see a woman obviously looking for someone she might recognize. She thought it might be Joy who would probably be concerned about whether she was still coming. *"That's Joy, all right,"* Shellie said in a low voice.

"I'll be right back," Joy said to Peter and the two women. She decided to walk toward Shellie after she was quite sure it was her in the distance.

When Shellie saw Joy she began to smile. She was happy to see her friend and knew at that very moment the trip she had waited so patiently for was going to finally become a reality.

Shellie and Joy immediately hugged each other. Joy could feel Shellie relax as they embraced.

"Shellie, you know you made me worry," Joy said with a little anxiety in her voice.

"I'm sorry for being so late, Joy. My family was not real pleased about me taking this trip on such short notice. I asked Roy to drop me off just to keep from hearing it. I love my family, but sometimes..." Shellie said, stopping in mid-sentence.

"Well put your family out of your mind, Shellie. This trip is about you having some fun," Joy said, trying to reassure her friend about her decision. "You *deserve* this cruise. You also look very nice in that suit."

With hair tied back in a small knot, Shellie looked like a flight attendant in her cream-colored suit and matching ankle strapped shoes.

"I know I deserve this cruise, Joy, but it's not easy for me. My family depends on me for so much," Shellie said.

"I'm glad you can at least admit it."

"I can't deny it. That's for sure. But...hey...I'm here and I can't wait to get on that plane!" Shellie said quite anxiously.

"That's the right spirit, girlfriend," Joy said. "But tell me...why do our men have to get so weak when it comes to not having us around? Peter was telling me how depressed he was going to be until I came back home. What are we going to do with them?"

"I have no idea. Let's not worry about it now cause *we're* going on this cruise, not them!" Shellie exclaimed.

Joy walked Shellie back to where the others were seated. Hailey and Monique said their hellos and gave her a hug. Peter shook her hand and welcomed her as well.

"Peter plans to stay until our plane takes off," Joy said, pointing out a seat for Shellie to take.

Joy was amazed at the number of people who had now gathered at their gate. An announcement was made. All passengers would be boarding the plane for Cincinnati soon. The stranger would be boarding as well.

two

We're All Here!

Two Delta flights,

one from Indianapolis and the other out of Baltimore, were scheduled to land in Cincinnati on Sunday morning. The four would finally be united with the last person of their cruising party, and that was LaNae.

Joy and Monique both screamed when they saw LaNae sitting in the boarding area for the connecting nonstop flight to New Orleans. LaNae screamed as well, as the three hugged each other and wiped away very emotional tears, which always flowed following one of their reunions. Joy introduced Hailey and Shellie to LaNae. She remembered them from NTM when she worked at the Indianapolis site. The two women thought LaNae's face looked familiar as well. Joy suggested that they all not worry about their families, nor be concerned about what might be going on back home. Everyone agreed and then they high fived each other right before they boarded the plane for New Orleans. The gate attendant checked passenger boarding passes and confirmed seat assignments. The five excited women walked down the boarding ramp, laughing and joking about what each was going to do during the seven-day cruise. LaNae, Monique, and Joy all sat together in the fourth row. Joy asked for the window seat. Shellie and Hailey sat separately two rows back and across from each other. Both women also had window seats.

The stranger also boarded the plane for New Orleans. He purposely let three passengers walk in front of him in case Joy might recognize him from the gate in Indianapolis. Good, he thought. Joy still had no idea how closely he watched her every move. He noticed how content she was with her friends. She laughed and smiled fondly with them. Each woman was obviously very special to her. He could say that she almost glowed in their presence. He watched them high five each other before the gate attendant announced that they would be boarding passengers for the two-hour New Orleans flight. He was flying first class, but he decided to board the plane after Joy. Being the last person to board, he could see exactly where she was seated. New Orleans was his final destination.

"We are about forty miles outside the New Orleans airport. The current temperature is eighty-one degrees, and the skies are mostly sunny with a southwest wind of ten miles per hour. At this time I'd like to ask the flight attendants to prepare for landing," said the Captain to passengers on board the Delta flight out of Cincinnati.

A few minutes later, a Black flight attendant with a British accent began speaking: *"On behalf of the Captain*

*and the crew, it was our pleasure to have you on board
Delta Airlines. We will be taxiing for a few minutes after
we touch down so please keep your seat belts fastened
until the aircraft comes to a complete stop. The local time
this morning is ten-twenty. Again, we thank you for flying
Delta and enjoy your stay in New Orleans."*

No one sings the blues in New Orleans with its Creole
cuisine, entertainment, and architectural ambiance. The French
Quarter has antique stores, horse-drawn carriage rides, trol-
ley cars, and lots of *live* music in the streets.

"We're here!" the five women screamed as they stood
together locked arm in arm in the New Orleans airport.

"Which way is the baggage claim in this airport? I
have never been here. Has anyone been here, Joy?" Hailey
asked, looking at all the airport signs.

"No...this is a first-time visit for all of us," Joy reminded
Hailey.

"There are signs all over the place! All we need to do
is read them," Monique said, pointing to a sign nearby that
indicated baggage claim was down one level from where they
were.

After the five successfully retrieved their luggage among
the many suitcases, trunks, and bags moving along the winding baggage claim lane, they spotted the cruise line attendant
holding a sign, who led them back up to the first floor of the
airport.

Outside the airport terminal several large buses were
waiting to pick them up along with others to transport them

and their luggage to the pier where the shipped was docked. A ramp was extended to the pier and the passengers were allowed to board the ship. Luggage was labeled before loading and stored in a stateroom aboard the ship for the required U.S. Customs' check. Later, all luggage was claimed by owners or taken directly to the cabins upon request.

Serenade the Seas cruise ship was operated by the Majestic Cruise Line. It was scheduled to depart at four in the afternoon for its two ports of call. The ship was about seven hundred and twenty-eight feet long. The ship had a staff of six hundred and sixty to serve the passengers on her eight decks, some of which were appropriately named after a geographic seas. The seven hundred cabins came in outside and inside grades, and depending on your category, each had a different room layout. The cabins of the five women were primarily located on the Mediterranean and Baltic Sea Decks.

The two ports of call for *Serenade the Seas* gave the passengers the opportunity for some shopping, sightseeing, and maximum appreciation of Mexico's white sandy beaches, coral reefs, and inland lagoons. The cruise included four fun days at sea! The ship was scheduled to return to New Orleans Sunday at eight o'clock in the morning.

Shellie had to use two frames of film in her camera to photograph the entire length of the forty-seven-thousand-plus gross tonnage ship, a view of the front half was in one frame, and the back half was in the other frame. The ship's porthole windows looked like the size of quarters from where the five were standing on the pier enjoying the view.

"This cruise is just what we all need!" Joy said, staring in awe at the view of the one thousand, four hundred and fifty-passenger ship. The others were overwhelmed by the view as well. The ship was truly an amazing sight of beauty!

"The brochure my travel agent sent me said meals and snacks are served daily along with those late night buffets!" LaNae exclaimed. "I think I also read that we have dinner with the ship's captain on our last night."

Serenade the Seas had seating for groups of four or more in either of her two dining rooms on the Middle Deck. The "Garden of Eden," had a more elegant formal decor than the classy dinner atmosphere provided in the "Caribbean Gem" dining room. Hundreds are served per their request of an early or late meal seating. Main seating was between six and six-thirty and late seating was between eight and eight-thirty. Early lunch seating was at noon and late seating began at one-thirty. Open seating for breakfast was from seven to nine, and buffet breakfasts, lunches, and dinners were always available.

"The only thing that sparked my interest was reading about the night activity...the bars, the dancing...the casinos," Monique said almost discounting the importance of what LaNae had just said.

Nighttime entertainment options on board *Serenade the Seas* ranged from Latin or disco dancing in the "OZ Club," a hot-and-happening place on Red Sea Deck. Or there was always live evening big band music or single person acts performing in the huge lounge and bar area called the "Emerald Palace Lounge." It was located on the Main Deck.

"...And don't forget we can go sightseeing in Mexico when we get off the ship, girls," Hailey said, thinking to herself about the opportunity to appreciate the people as well as the scenery.

After boarding the ship, the five women walked together leisurely (but not on all eight decks). The ship had two fresh water swimming pools, an indoor and outdoor Jacuzzi on the Caribbean Deck, and a movie theater on Baltic Sea Deck. The beauty salon and plenty of onboard daytime activities were held inside and outside on the Main Deck. A poster announcing the very popular daily aerobic classes was hanging in the Main Deck activity display cabinet. Classes for advance and beginners/intermediates, and a seniors class were offered daily at scheduled times. All passengers were welcome to join in for some fitness fun. The gymnasium and spa were located on the Mediterranean Deck, which overlooked one of the two pools.

The five sat talking in an empty recreation room just off the Main Deck lobby. The Main Deck was lined with boutique shops, champagne fountains, chairs, and winding barstools. Patrons could sit and enjoy the sun's rays through the atrium glass windows during the day and a view of the moon and the stars at night when the Emerald Palace Lounge came to life. It was there that Joy shared a souvenir gift idea with them that she thought they would all appreciate. She had read in one of the cruise brochures that their ship had a T-shirt boutique. She asked each of the women if they wanted to select a personal day of the week to wear a T-shirt specially made for them with some inscription. On that woman's special day, the other four would come up with the wording for the T-shirt, and contribute an equal amount toward its total cost. The saying would appear on the front of the T-shirt and the person's name would be printed on the back in large letters. Joy had spoken to the vendor earlier during their mini-tour to work out the details regarding when to place the order and pickup times. Shellie picked Monday, tomorrow's first full day on the ship. Monique chose Tuesday. Hailey just *had* to have Wednesday. And LaNae chose Thursday, of course, because that was her birthday. Joy wanted Friday of their cruise.

After Joy's T-shirt idea was agreed upon, the women decided they would go to their cabins to freshen up and change clothes for lunch on the deck. They were going to meet again but outside on the Middle Deck for *Serenade's* "Set Sail

Barbeque" cookout at the "Sandy Beach Bar-n-Grill," where breakfast, light lunches, and buffet dinners were served to passengers who didn't want to dine in a formal setting.

The temperature was in the mid-eighties and it was time to undock from the pier. Actual departure time was at four in the afternoon. As *Serenade the Seas* pulled away from the New Orleans' pier, many passengers continued to "pig out" on the grilled burgers, fried food, and the well stocked salad and pasta bar. Others on shore waved farewell and wished a safe return to the crew and passengers.

Hailey, as she had mentioned that morning in Indianapolis, continued to look for a cute cabin boy to carry her luggage. Several had offered to help her. She did look a little helpless. And she really was, but only because she no longer wanted to walk in those heels. She was even more inconvenienced by the fact that she might even end up pulling her own rather large pieces of luggage through some of the more narrower walkways on the ship. (Luckily, her suitcases had wheels.)

After she turned down the second offer for assistance, a young Italian cabin steward about Hailey's age, light brown complexion, dark hair, and deep set eyes, walked toward her.

With a thick accent he said, "You look like you could use some help, ma'am."

"Yes, I can. This ship is quite large and I'm confused. I'm not really sure where my cabin is," Hailey whined, now appearing to Joy and the others to be even more helpless than she really was.

"We're going to our cabin, Hailey. You look like you have everything under control," Joy said, sneaking Hailey a quick thumbs up. Monique and LaNae were trying hard not to laugh. They couldn't believe this girl and her antics. She hadn't been on the ship for more than an hour and here she was already playing up to this young man who hung on her every word like she was a piece of raw meat and he was a hungry lion.

The four women had already asked for directions to their cabins. Monique walked around the ship going up elevators and stairways like she knew exactly where she was going. Shellie soon located her single inside cabin and Monique found the room she, Joy, and LaNae were sharing, which was an outside cabin. Both were located on the Mediterranean Deck.

Shellie unpacked and immediately changed from her suit into a pair of yellow shorts with a matching top and sandals. She didn't feel like putting on anything too flamboyant following all of the airport walking and plane shuffling. Being comfortable was her priority at this point. She'd leave all those flashy clothes for that Hailey girl to wear. She seemed to be a nice woman, but she tried too hard to get attention from men.

When LaNae, Monique, and Joy entered their cabin, they were somewhat impressed. There were twin bunk beds, and another single twin-size bed just off an adjacent wall. A lamp and small table and chair were located in the corner between the two beds. Up against the other corner wall of the room was a small three-cushion couch and table with a plastic flower centerpiece. They had one moderately sized closet, and the bathroom consisted of a sink, a commode, and a adequate-size shower stall.

The three also changed into shorts outfits and left their room. Anxious to eat buffet style lunch out on the ship's deck, they decided to unpack later. They wondered for a brief moment if Shellie and Hailey had already gone up to eat.

Hailey finally got to her room on the Baltic Deck. The cabin steward struggled, but he did manage to get her luggage through the narrow doorway. Hailey thanked him politely, and offered him a tip, which he graciously accepted. Then he stood there for a brief moment hands in his pocket as if Hailey was going to invite him to stay. She smiled and then turned her back on him, beginning to unpack her things. He awkwardly and abruptly excused himself and left.

Her cabin had a bed, a small light table and chair, a mirror over the dresser, and a bathroom with a shower. The room was an outside cabin with a small port side window from which she could see the emergency lifeboats hanging off the ship.

Hailey promised herself that she would definitely make sure she enjoyed this cruise. She quickly put on a pastel peach sundress with an open back. Hailey figured because it was lined no one could see through it, which was fundamental because Hailey very rarely wore underwear.

By the time she unpacked and got dressed, Hailey was quite hungry. She was even more eager for excitement and the opportunity to bring one of her many fantasies to reality. She headed upstairs without a clue about how to get to the ship's deck for lunch.

Another passenger managed to get a direct flight to New Orleans. Bold and determined to take the same cruise as Joy and her sisterfriends, he rode on the second bus that transported passengers to the pier; Joy and her friends were on the first bus. It was easy to watch Joy from a distance through his dark sunglasses as she boarded her bus. However, once on he got on the cruise ship, he knew he had to be more inconspicuous. He didn't want to spoil his plans.

On the ship, he retrieved his luggage and carry-on bag. As he walked to his cabin, he was content with having reached his final destination safely. The fact that Joy was traveling with her friends was a good thing. He now began to plot what he might do to arrange for them to finally see each other on the ship. Being a man he knew that many like him would want to get near her as well. Yes, many lions, tigers, and bears would want Joy's attention. When he saw Joy for the first time, he was paralyzed by her beauty. The need to be near her now was very powerful.

*Lions and tigers and bears...*just another set of collective words to refer to men or to describe the way they act. To put it plainly...all men *aren't dogs!* Some men are proud, courageous *lion kings*, some radiate their presence with brilliant, bold *tiger stripes*, and others are always there to generously give the most gentle, carassing *bear hugs*.

three
The Gold Medal

Lions and tigers and bears want the gold medal, which is that special woman who is all that a man would ever want her to be and one who gives her man all he would ever need. She would have no problem falling in love with her man. And he would certainly be in awe of her.

As fitness director aboard *Serenade the Seas* ship, Sidney Masters at forty-seven knows all to well that he looks thirty-seven. More tiger in nature, Sidney's physical attractiveness in conjunction with his magnetic personality, has made him a true charmer upon sight alone. Sidney knows he's made many a heart skip a beat. His voice and alluring mannerisms have allowed him to capitalize on the opposite sex. Sidney would never waste his assets on a man. He is quite the gentleman at six feet four, two hundred fifty-five pounds. The respect he commands has kept him at the front of the line to meet women of all "shades of beauty," including both eligible and ineligible interested parties.

It was Monday, the ship's first full day at sea. The ship's workout and recreation room on the Main Deck provided lots of space for Sidney to take good care of about a hundred passengers who were interested in fitness while they were on their cruise. All of his classes were coed, but more than two-thirds consisted of women. He could accommodate up to about thirty-five persons per class. He had a senior citizens aerobics class at eight-thirty in the morning, an advanced class at nine forty-five, and a beginners/intermediate class at three-fifteen in the afternoon. Most of the time he coordinated the exercise activities for one or two special groups on board the ship. Sidney loved his job simply because he loved being around people, mainly women. Women take more cruises then men so Sidney had managed to stay employed in the cruise line business for many years. This job had certainly given him an edge on how to wine and dine women on land and at sea. Entertaining one or two women after a workout with champagne was usually on his agenda. His mission: to keep his charter (mainly the women) satisfied. Even if this meant he had to work in a few extra one-on-one sessions.

Well today's morning group of about fifteen seniors was no treat. Sidney was having an unusually boring day. Some women take cruises more often when they turn sixty. They never tire of paying to travel in style or to be cared for in style, especially if it's done in Sidney style. This sixty plus group wasn't too old but their "Hello Sidneys" just didn't have the same effect on him as that delivered by those younger by ten or fifteen years. Sidney knew all women were beautiful in their own way. He also knew they wanted his attention up close and personal. But when a woman is older, with a wrinkle or two, a bit slower, and just too color coordinated, she is just that—old and not as exciting as she used to be. The women in this morning's exercise class were no sights to linger on, but they were probably definitely *lookers* in their time. Sidney just couldn't give them the benefit of the doubt now. Nevertheless, he was still in the driver's seat of this scenario, and he knew he couldn't leave them unfulfilled. So he made himself get into character. If he wanted to be able to play the game, he'd better at least get into the mood, he thought. That was the first step.

"Okay, ladies…let's BEND to the left, then BEND to the right, DOWN OVER to the FLOOR, and UP on FOUR!" Sidney shouted in his powerful, deep baritone voice. "Once again…one, two, three…and BEND to the left, then BEND to the right, and DOWN to the FLOOR, and UP on FOUR!" Boy oh boy, he thought, this group sucks.

The sixty- and seventy-year-old ladies were awkward, short, tall, some were a little shapely, and others had more pudgy bodies. The more ample bodies had waistlines that were hidden by fuller breasts and child-bearing stomachs. Others just had wide hips. Most of the women covered themselves with oversized tops and warmup pants and jacket sets. When they bent at the waist to attempt to touch the floor on Sidney's count of three, the ones who hesitated with effort almost fell over. Most of them were able to come up on his count of four and stretch high and tall as he capably did. Nevertheless, they did all manage to stay on some kind of rhythmic count.

Everyone, that is, EXCEPT for Mrs. Gertie (short for Gertrude) Needles, a widow who was eighty plus years old. Gertie almost fell over twice when she bent her body to the left and then to the right. It was rather comical. She couldn't keep up with Sidney's count, and she looked like she was trying so hard. She was the oldest member of this workout ensemble. She even had a little sweat on her brow if you looked close enough.

"Now I hope I don't need to slow this exercise down," Sidney said almost laughing when he glanced at Gertie. "You ladies seem to be struggling. We can't go any slower. AND we have five more sets left to do."

"Sidney, will you come over here, please?" announced Mrs. Janeen McClaine in a low, alluring, but not exactly seductive, voice. It was more of a command than a request. Janeen McClaine had been trying to get Sidney to help her since the exercise session began. If she had her way, she'd have Sidney help her on *every* exercise. All she really wanted was to be touched by him. In all honesty, it could be just about anyone. And it didn't matter where she was touched either. Her one and only husband for the past forty-five years had stopped touching her many, many years ago and a doctor's visit was just that...a doctor's visit. Except for that one office visit with Dr. Richard Prickard. She had to admit that she did get aroused a little during one of his examinations.

"I can't seem to bend low enough. Should I try to touch the floor? Am I doing this exercise right?" she asked. Her questions were asked in an attempt to get Sidney to give her some attention. She wore an aqua blue warmup suit with a matching cap. The jacket was unzipped just low enough to reveal her white fitted shirt and what Sidney would be willing to bet were true D cups. No surgical enhancements. They were real. They looked real and Sidney would probably get the chance to see if they felt real.

This woman is getting on my nerves, Sidney thought. She's probably around sixty-five, although she looks ten years younger. Her body doesn't look that bad either when you consider her age. Black women never look their age. But I wish this classy broad would just stop trying so hard. I will probably get together with her later to give her some real personal help. She's such an easy catch. They all make it so easy for me. It's really a shame...but am I making anyone do anything they don't wanna do? No. They do it to themselves. I just reap the benefits and they do too!

"Now Janeen, you know you have the right moves. I really don't have to check on you," Sidney said a little flirtatiously but not in his best or most convincing manner.

"I'll watch, but I'm not helping you. There are no short cuts. This exercise is easy and you know the routine better than me." Sidney's voice was authoritatively dry.

He walked over to Janeen whose very attractive smile seemed to broaden the closer he got. She was standing in the middle of the second row. There were five women in each row. The group of fifteen stood in a horse shoe shape, which enabled them to have a clear view of Sidney's entire body. They liked what they saw. It was hard not to appreciate the view of Sidney in his black one-piece body builder workout suit, which revealed much of his muscular chest and arms, along with the other parts of his firm muscular body.

Sidney stood behind Janeen just close enough to brush up against her backside *very* lightly. He learned this technique and had perfected it himself from practice. But Sidney wasn't going to touch her because he knew that was what she wanted. He didn't want to touch her just now. He knew he could affect her more by not touching her. Leaving someone in a state of *wanting* to be touched always had a more lasting effect.

Janeen's entire body quivered in anticipation of what *she* thought *he* was going to do. Her visual and sensual fantasy was probably along the lines of how good it would feel to have Sidney's hands touching her shoulders first, then sliding down to her arms and fingertips. He'd have to hold her at the waist to help position her to bend correctly. Janeen would be willing to pay Sidney a whole lot for some of *that* kind of attention. But it was not going to happen today, not now at least. Sidney was not in the mood.

The other ladies were now pointing and whispering to each other about how foolish Janeen looked. They knew she was teasing Sidney, and they even seemed to be waiting to see how he was going to respond. You see, secretly, they all wanted a turn at flirting with the master.

Later that afternoon, between classes, Sidney Masters stopped at the Emerald Palace Lounge to have a drink. His senior's morning class had the least number of people. His nine forty-five advanced class was larger than he expected, and he thought his three-fifteen beginners/intermediate class would be even larger. The advanced class was a dedicated group, most of whom said they enjoyed the workout and would return the next day.   Sidney's childhood friend from New Jersey was the head bartender of the Emerald Palace Lounge. His name was Howard Zeus Maxwell and most people called him by his middle name. Sidney knew he'd needed a drink and figured he'd also have the listening ear of his best friend, Howie (which was what *Sidney* always called him) to vent to about the day's *uneventful* happenings.

"I just finished my first two classes. Fix me a drink, Howie," Sidney said dryly.

"The regular, man?" Howard said, a little concerned about his friend's mood. "What's up with you? Dare I ask why you are so down?"

"Yeah, the usual, How. And you don't wanna know."

"Grand Marnier on the rocks coming right up," Howard said, reaching for a glass to fill it with ice. "And man, I do want to know so talk to me."

"You know, Howie, I may not necessarily be attracted to every woman I meet. But did I ever tell you about this woman I ran into in New York during my layover in March?"

"No, Sid, you didn't. Is this one of those stories I'm going wish I didn't hear?"

"No, Howie. You can handle this one, trust me."

"Okay, if you say so. Let's hear it, man."

"Well, this woman sort of got to me like no other woman has. She was self-assured and seemed to enjoy my company simply because she could. There was no neediness or insecurity about her."

"Sounds like the perfect woman, if any exist."

"No, this one had some issues all right, but she never made a point to burden me with them. She's the private, Ms. Handle It type. You know how they are."

"Yeah, those are the ones who never look my way."

"Well, you have to be able to stand up to them. If you are the least bit intimidated, they won't give you the time of day."

"I guess that explains my bum luck. Here I thought it was my breath or something," Howard said as he wiped the bar where Sidney was sitting.

"No, Howie, remind me and I'll tell you what it really is someday, okay?'

"Don't hold your breath, Sid. I won't be ready for that lecture for while."

"Anyway, let me finish, man. I just don't understand why she's on my mind today. I thought about her a lot after we went our separate ways."

"Then why didn't you call her?"

"We didn't exchange numbers. I don't even know where she works. It was just supposed to be a quick thing. We were just kickin' it for a day or two."

"Oh..." Howard said, thinking how fortunate Sidney was to have a woman who wanted to *kick it* with him. He would love to be able to kick it with one of Sidney's women. Just one or two of them at the same time.

"For some reason, I feel like I'm almost being willed by some force to think about her. It's like she's close to me in some way, which is both weird and impossible."

"Just how much do you think about her?"

"Not very often. It's just been a little more intense for the past month or so."

"What did you two do for that day or two?"

"Man, why do you want to know all my business?"

"Because I can ask and you can answer."

"Well...we just spent some quality time together. One very late night talking, and then one full day with each other until the next morning."

"Doesn't seem like you to fall for a woman after a day and a half, Sidney."

"I'm not sure what's come over me. I don't believe I've actually fallen for this woman, or really *ever* fallen for anyone for that matter. I always want the option of letting them go, particularly when *I'm* ready."

"I *see* your point."

"Since that nine-year live-in mate *finally* decided to make her move—mainly out of my house, clothes and all!—I vowed I'd never let myself get too close to anyone."

"Sid, you shouldn't make vows like that based on one relationship."

"You mean one long relationship, don't you?" Sidney asked.

"I guess a long relationship *can* make a difference."

"It does, believe me."

"Whatever you say, Sid."

"Now you know, the only reason I teach aerobics on a cruise ship is to be around women. In fact, working in the cruise industry is the ideal place for men like us because it's the very outlet we need to keep our life balanced, occupied, *and* exciting."

"I know what you mean. Being a bartender has its perks, too. And don't forget the exotic places we get to visit."

"The opportunity to travel is one thing...but coming in contact with as many women as possible in one setting is another. If other men only knew the number of women we meet on a weekly basis."

"Daily basis, man. Shiit, they would kill to do what we do," Howard said.

"Shiit, Howie, you'd kill to do what *I* do."

"What about what I do?"

"Just what do you do, Howie?"

"Man, why do you call me, Howie? Everyone else calls me Zeus."

"Cause I've known your ass since you were *little* Howie," Sidney said as he indicated a height of two feet with his right hand level with the barstool beside him. "Do you want me to start calling you that more often?"

"No, Sid. That's all right. You can call me Howard, but if you can manage, use the name Zeus every once in awhile, particularly if you see me in the company of a beautiful woman. I would appreciate it, okay?"

"Yeah, okay, How...I mean Zeus...I won't try to intentionally mess up your play or embarrass you. You're the man when it comes to the ladies. You make those exotic drinks for these women that not only taste good, but *look good* with all the neat things you can do with cherries, limes, olives, and those ribbons and strings and things. They seem to do the trick cause your bar is always hopping with business. People really seem to enjoy your company, or maybe it's just the drinks?" Sidney said, teasing his friend, now.

"I don't know, Howie. Just what do you put in your drinks?" Sidney said apparently thinking for the first time that Howard *was* that gifted in his profession.

"That's my secret, workout boy. You get your chance after you loosen up their bodies, right? Well, I get mine after I loosen up their lips and relax their minds. A drink will do it every time."

"I loosen up plenty of bodies, but I ain't nobody's boy," Sidney shot back at Howard.

"Okay, I'm sorry 'bout the boy thang, but after a few of my 'emotion potions,' woman tell me everything. Then I can make my move."

"It's your 'emotion potions.'"

"Yes, Sid, my man. I've been checkin' out the fresh meat that's come on board. They're a little jet lagged today, but by tomorrow, they'll start to realize that they're on OUR ship and R&R is the operative way of life out on the seas."

"R&R...what does that stand for...uh...Zeus?" Sidney said with a laugh.

"YOU don't *know*, Flirt Masters?"

"No, please enlighten me."

"Well, R&R means 'real and relaxin,' which is what you get when you hang out with real men like you and me, Sidney," Howard advised.

"Oh! So you think you and I are in the same league?" Sidney said not trying to sound too arrogant.

"Yeah, Sidney. I got your back, right? We look after each other."

"Yeah, Howie, but you know I operate alone. Not too many people get into my business cause I don't let them. You have special rights." Sidney meant that too.

"We go way back, Howard or Zeus...or whatever your name is," Sidney said. "But don't misinterpret our close friendship. I love you like a brother, my brotha. But I only tell you what I want you to know and invite you in my space when I wanna see your face. Otherwise, you'd be a pain in the ass like most people are to me anyway."

"I know...you like your space and for people to mind their own business. People are always trying to live off what's happening in someone else's life instead of making it happen for themselves."

"They sure do, Howard. People are lazy and always want to take the easy street. Men and women alike."

"I've been around you long enough, Sid, to stay out of your way. Haven't I?"

"Yes, you have, man." Sidney did appreciate the fact that they had remained friends for such a long time.

"I don't need to live through you, cause I got it that way with the women too," Howard said. He really could have it that way as he so aptly put it, if for one thing, he was a little more secure with himself and two, he didn't have unresolved issues from his childhood. Howard was raised by a very controlling father and therefore he grew up to be the type of man who can rarely say no to a woman. So if he ran into the wrong type of woman, she could easily take advantage of him. And the wrong type had done so. Howard had to learn the hard way. By age thirty-one, he had regained much of his self-esteem. With a few helpful tips from his friend Sidney, Howard managed to avoid women whose intent was to play games with his heart.

"So you think you got it that way with this new name and all? Just what's up with the name change, Howard? Didn't you start using it a few years ago?"

"Man, I've always used the name Zeus. I only started using it more often after I heard one of my women call me by it and I liked the way it sounded, especially when it was whispered in my ear just before ...uh...well you know what I mean."

"Whoa...give me a break, Zeus. Spare me the details of your sex life. Will you?" Sidney said as he finished his drink and stood up to leave.

"Okay, Sid, but trust me. The name works like a charm. What can I say?" Howard boasted.

"Well...you know the old saying: If it ain't broke, then why fix it. Live long and prosper with the women, almighty Zeus!" Sidney said humorously, trying to make the Vulcan sign with his fingers.

"...but just save some women for me!" Sidney yelled out from the recreation room off the ship's spacious Main Deck.

four
Secrets and Lies

Back in February, LaNae wrote Solomon about how she felt about him...well...how she felt about *them* and whether they should pursue a more definite relationship in some fashion. She had ended the letter by asking Solomon if he would consider going on this cruise. And Solomon, crazy enough to try to pull it off, had said yes. He had to tell his wife three BIG lies to keep the trip a secret. The first and most sinful lie was to tell her that NTM, his firm, was sending him to New Orleans to attend a national conference for purchasing agents. The second was just as immoral because he told her the conference would last an entire week. The third lie was telling his wife that his schedule would be so busy that he wouldn't have time to call her every day, adding that he would call her as the conference schedule permitted. (Now trying to avoid Joy and Monique on that ship for first day or two would keep him sorta busy, so perhaps this wasn't a complete lie?)

✴ four

Solomon's wife said it was all right if he didn't have time to call and that she wouldn't be upset if he didn't call. She was so used to him traveling that she told him to call her from the airport before he caught his connecting flight for home. If you really think about it, she is either a very trusting wife and doesn't need to worry about her husband's whereabouts, OR she has a hidden agenda of her own. Solomon, so caught up in his own lies, never gave his wife's response to his travel itinerary a second thought.

Solomon tried to remember when his relationship with LaNae caught fire once again. It was about a year and a half ago. And it took some time. He left NTM in Indianapolis to work in the Baltimore, Maryland, office, only to return after three weeks. He ended up missing LaNae more than he thought he ever would. He called her a couple of times long distance. She never returned his calls. Once he tried talking to Joy, her best friend. He asked Joy if she would persuade LaNae to call him back. Joy took pleasure in reminding Solomon that LaNae "IS grown," and can pretty much do whatever she wants with whomever she wants. Then she politely told Solomon that he needed to grow up and accept responsibility for the consequences of his action to leave Indianapolis in the first place. *And* she asked him if had forgotten the fact that he didn't really say goodbye to LaNae.

Solomon's next move was to write to LaNae. When she received the first envelope, she could tell it was just a card so she put it through her paper shredder without opening it. A second and third envelope (also with cards inside) followed over the next two and a half weeks. LaNae kept these (albeit, unread) in the center drawer of her desk. Her curiosity got the best of her when a fourth envelope arrived with her name and office address on it. She decided to open it because it wasn't a card this time. It was a letter. A four-page letter from Solomon.

Solomon wrote her about how much he loved her and that he hoped that they had something special enough for her to forgive him for his stupidity and for taking their relationship for granted. He apologized for not saying goodbye to her before he left. He explained that it was too painful to bring closure to their relationship (even though it should have ended many years ago). He told her that he concluded that if neither of them said goodbye then their relationship could never really be over. (He was obviously right about that.) He also told her that he was afraid of losing her as a friend. Basically he didn't have the balls to say goodbye. (Joy had already told LaNae that quite a few times. Monique had told her too.) Solomon went on to ask LaNae if she thought maybe their friendship was worth saving. He said he certainly thought it was. He ended his letter with "LU, Solomon."

LaNae was emotionally overwhelmed by his honesty. He had once again professed his love for her. His apology was a little weak, but hadn't he told her that he feared losing her? She decided to call him to see if he had balls enough to want to save their friendship at least. She was secretly hooked on him again, but she wasn't going to tell him how really hooked she was. She had no plans to tell Joy or Monique either.

When Solomon transferred back to NTM's office in Indianapolis, he continued to write and send LaNae discreet messages. His entire courtship to win LaNae back lasted about four months. Then one day LaNae decided that perhaps they could be good friends like they were from the start. She did have to remind him that what they did in the capacity of being friends would be different. Physical intimacy...well, it wasn't going to happen because it wasn't integral to their rekindled friendship. They also decided that if they didn't want ANY-ONE to know about them, then they could not be seen together at work. This friendship thing between her and Solomon was going to be their little *secret* and they were both pre-pared to *lie* to keep it that way.

LaNae and Solomon remained respectful of each other's space *and* spouses. They decided to never see or call each other if they were really weak or needy. That was a big challenge for LaNae. She knew it was an even bigger chal-lenge for Solomon. They both agreed that being "needy and greedy" would create a friendship that might make one party more dependent on the other, and this would be nothing but painful in the long run.

They managed to spend time together at public places in which no one would be able to assume that they were—together. They always drove separate cars. The public library was their favorite spot. Solomon always considered the li-brary to be an erotic place for them to go, particularly if they found a secluded area. They would sit on carpeted floor and act like they were reading a book or they would even some-times actually discuss a book they had both read. They ulti-mately got closer, not necessarily physically, but definitely emotionally. They would frequently share a quick kiss every now and then or give each other big hugs as long they knew they were not being watched and no one familiar was in close proximity to them.

Other favorite get-together spots were plays and con-certs. Solomon (and sometimes LaNae) would purchase tick-ets (always with cash) with the same seat number but in two different rows; LaNae would either sit directly behind him or he would sit in front of her. That seating setup allowed either of them, depending on who sat in front of whom, to dis-creetly *touch* the shoulder or neck of the other or to whisper just about anything in the other's ear. It was usually more of a turn-on for LaNae than Solomon. They always got up during the intermission to prudently mingle (together, that is) along with everyone else.

After about six months with Solomon as a "secret" friend, LaNae received a long awaited promotion. She knew NTM would ask her to relocate to the Baltimore office (the same office from which Solomon had just returned). LaNae accepted the offer. She told Joy it was a career move she couldn't afford to pass up and that her husband supported her all the way. Joy suspected that her move might have something to do with Solomon but she didn't know how. All Joy knew was that Solomon was here in Indianapolis with LaNae. There was a strong scent of deception in the air. Joy thought if LaNae moved to Baltimore then perhaps she might have a better chance of getting Solomon finally out of her life for good.

LaNae and Solomon had already discussed the possibility of LaNae moving to Baltimore. They agreed that the move would be a good thing to slow down the pace of what was happening between them. They weren't planning to end the close friendship they had managed to nurture once again. Neither had any intentions of giving the other up. In fact, keeping in touch long distance might prove to be a better arrangement for them after all. They could look forward to their long distance talks on the phone (from his office or hers, that is) and still manage to take care of their families and professional careers...until the opportunity for this cruise came up. Then things changed...

All along, LaNae, in great denial for about the hundredth time about her real feelings for Solomon, knew she was falling again hard and fast. She knew things weren't perfect in her own household. Tolerable, yes. But perfect, no. She had never really considered being without her husband, Freddy. Ever. She was committed. Not faithfully in all cases, but committed nonetheless. So when she began to think about how she really felt about her husband and how she really felt about Solomon, things were getting a bit confusing. Her priorities to her family were shifting and a new found commitment to be happy was moving in fast. She decided to write Solomon and ask him to join her on the cruise and they, together, would work out the details of their future. She was about to greet life head on at forty. Would it be with or without Solomon? She just wasn't sure.

And Solomon wasn't sure how or where he was going to hide all day Sunday while he was on this cruise ship called *Serenade the Seas.* If LaNae's very best friends, Joy and Monique, saw him they would freak. He and LaNae had planned to keep their little secret, just that, for at least the first two days at sea. After that they would meet each other when they wanted and if the two women saw them, then it wouldn't be a secret anymore. Part one of the master plan required that Solomon fly out of Indianapolis to Cincinnati on Friday, instead of Saturday, which was when Joy and Monique were leaving. Leaving on Friday would give Solomon an extra day in New Orleans and he practically begged LaNae to fly in early and join him. LaNae explained that not only would she have to lie to her husband about why she had to leave a day ahead of schedule, but that the plan (Joy's plan, that is), was that she and Monique would fly to Cincinnati, meet up with LaNae there, and then the three would all fly into New Orleans together. If LaNae was not on that Cincinnati flight, Joy would be highly upset to say the least. LaNae didn't want to be questioned, mainly because she wouldn't be able to answer to the utmost satisfaction of her controlling, yet concerned sisterfriend, Joy. So…Solomon's plans were quickly scrapped. He was quite disappointed. Nevertheless, part one went smoothly and Solomon got to New Orleans a day earlier than everyone else.

Part two of the master plan involved Solomon board-ing the ship either before LaNae and her cruising buddies had boarded or after them. Solomon decided he wanted to board after them. He went to the pier on Friday and made some inquiries about the boarding time. He knew when LaNae and the others would arrive in New Orleans and approximately when they would be transported from the airport to the ship's docking area. Solomon planned to leave his hotel early enough to give him time to get to the dock and still board the ship later without being seen. Part two was carried out without a hitch.

Now, when it came to part three, Solomon had to be extra careful. By mid-afternoon Sunday, he hadn't seen LaNae or any of her friends from NTM. The ship sparkled with activ-ity. Luckily, only Joy and Monique knew what he looked like. He had heard about the barbeque at the Sandy Beach Bar-n-Grill on the Middle Deck and assumed that the women would want to eat outside on the patio. He ate in the Carribean Gem dining room.

On Monday, it was harder for Solomon to pull off this hide-but-seek-out-LaNae game because the ship was at sea for the entire day. He didn't know where LaNae would be on the ship, but there was a perfectly good chance that he might run into her or *them* and vice versa. Therefore, Solomon, who rarely ate breakfast, slept in late that morning. He also avoided hanging around that Emerald Palace Lounge on Main Deck, and the pools on Caribbean Deck. When he was out-side, he stayed in the more secluded areas of the ship like Baltic Sea Deck, and the Upper Deck for sun bathers, where at least he knew LaNae, Monique, and Joy would have no reason to be. Or he stayed inside his cabin, but not too often.

✱ four

He was also prepared to eat alone in the Caribbean Gem again, sitting at a table in the back. He did a rather good job of keeping himself scarce on the ship. However, he didn't plan to do it much longer.

Solomon knew he had to be hooked more than ever to agree to a stunt like this one. *"I am out of control,"* he said aloud to himself while sipping on a drink at one of the less populated bars on the ship's top deck. It was around seven on Monday evening. He figured LaNae and her friends would be at dinner around this time. He was safe for now. He loved LaNae, but this business of sneaking around on a cruise ship was a little bit crazy. He was over forty, which meant he was too old to behave in this immature way. *What's love got to do with it, Tina? A whole lot in this case*, he thought.

Solomon's obsession with LaNae was something he never did want to harness, but their relationship defintely needed harnessing. What was it about LaNae that made him do just about anything to be near her? Only Solomon can answer that. The two were very close at one time. Lovers in fact. It all got started more than ten years ago. They just clicked and came to enjoy each other's company. They were true friends in the beginning. Once they entered the forbidden friendship zone, and began to develop those strong feelings for each other, that's when their long serious affair began.

Sure, Solomon had some regrets about lying to his wife, but she usually accommodated much of his behavior. It was easy for Solomon to lie because his wife was still unconditionally committed to loving him. After several years of marriage, if their relationship had a lot of unresolved issues, then Solomon could probably lie to his wife more often and have even less guilt. He wasn't actually burdened with guilt now. They were very relaxed about their marriage, but not to the point that either took the other for granted. Solomon had just never had a reason to doubt his wife's love for him. He took care of her and his family. He loved his wife, you could say, at least, in a functional way. Why? Mainly because he knew she would never leave him.

On the not so positive side, some lions and tigers and bears (men, that is) usually need some kind of secure relationship in their life. They might be willing to risk it all by having an affair or a brief fling as long as they really know deep inside their hearts that their significant other will never leave them. Even the men who feel trapped in their marriages, and Solomon did sometimes, won't stray too far from home. They don't want to give "home" totally up. They just need an outlet or a few outlets to keep things exciting for them. Having someone on the side can make the homefront more tolerable. Some guys are visual so being able to look at other women is enough for them. Other men go a little beyond that and will always keep one or two special friends in their life, which is probably why Solomon got involved with LaNae years ago in the first place.

five
Shellie's Day

It was seven-thirty

Monday morning, and also Shellie's special day. She woke up
not feeling special, but a little tired from her flight and slightly
apprehensive about her decision to take this cruise. She hated
to second guess herself. Besides that, it was always after the
fact. *Why can't I make a major decision to do something
and just accept it for what it is.* She prayed silently with her
eyes closed while laying in the twin-size cabin bed. Nothing
ever went wrong for Shellie when she made a decision to do
something. Unless you count the fact that she always felt *wrong*
inside. This morning was no exception. Shellie felt wrong
about leaving her husband...she felt wrong about leaving her
children...she felt selfish about putting her needs first. And
she felt *plain ole wrong* for wanting to relax and enjoy this
cruise, which was what her subconscious mind was screaming
out for her to do.

✻ five

It was more than just the decision to take the cruise. It was about having to decide about which direction she wanted to go with her marriage and her life. It was also about returning home after the cruise and having to actually communicate that decision to her family. Then ultimately it was being able to personally live with the decision she had made. Shellie had made no decisions yet simply because without a calm state of mind she couldn't begin to relax enough to do what she came on the cruise to do in the first place. This was truly a viscious cycle, and she had to break it in order to make the right decision for everyone involved.

Deep breathe...deep breathe, Shellie repeated to herself having sat up in her bunk. She took three long deep breaths. This seemed to relieve her of most of the initial anxiety she felt. It was working now. She felt better, stronger, and less vulnerable and fragile. *If a decision is what I have to make, then I'm going to make one*, she said to herself. *I can do it, but not now. What's the rush. I have seven days to decide what I'm going to do, don't I?*

She got up to take a shower, hoping it would reduce the rest of her anxiety and allow her to embrace this new day—and not half-heartedly. After her shower, she began to get dressed. She felt like wearing something loose. She was going out to the pool to lie in the sun and she wanted to be comfortable. Perhaps a small outside breeze might blow the stress away and clear her mind. She opened the small cabin closet, and reached for her long, off-the-shoulder coverall made of white gauze fabric. Underneath this she decided to wear a high cut one-piece white swim suit in case she felt an urge to swim later that morning. You could barely see the outline of her shapely body. Shellie left her cabin and headed toward the dining room for breakfast. She had managed to work up an appetite following her morning of tension and worry.

"So what are we going to put on a T-shirt for your friend Shellie? It's her day today and we're supposed to come up with a saying that's appropriate for her, right?" LaNae asked Joy as she and Monique laid fully awake in their cabin beds. It was just a few minutes after eight in the morning.

"I haven't thought of anything yet. It doesn't have to be anything elaborate. I know she's thinking about her marriage a lot these days so whatever we do we could think along those lines, maybe," Joy said.

"Did she really want to come on this cruise?" LaNae asked.

"Yes, she did. I just want her to be happy and enjoy it," Joy said.

"Then we'll just have to make sure she has a good time," Monique said being in full agreement with Joy. "But Joy, your friend seems like one of those take-care-of-it wives without a life of her own," Monique said not intending to be critical of Shellie.

"Now don't you be insensitive about her, Monique. Everyone has issues to deal with in their marriage. Even you," LaNae said in Shellie's defense.

"I know people go through things in a marriage, but you have to have a strong backbone to deal and some folk don't have what it takes. And, I don't mean to compare Black women to White women, but we are different when it comes to marriage and handling our affairs."

"You're right, Monique. But Shellie's situation is a little different. I'm not going to go into any details about her marriage because I don't know what their specific problems are. But I think handling anything in your marriage is about personal strength and the power within to survive," Joy said.

"I think so too. There are sistas out there who won't play any games with men and sistas who have breakdowns because their phones aren't ringing off the hook. They come in all ages and races," LaNae quickly said.

"Well, I suspect Shellie has a pretty sound foundation at home, but I have to tell you I don't know the full story," Joy said.

"I just hope she isn't out of it too much. I don't want any negative energy around me because it'll just bring my spirits down. I paid too much money for this trip. We all did!" Monique said looking at Joy.

"So, Joy, just what kind of saying can we put on her T-shirt, anyway?" Monique continued.

"I don't know, Monique. Something about what it takes to be a woman or wife. She seems to always have the strength to hang in there," Joy suggested.

"How 'bout..." Monique began to say.

"Now don't forget, whatever we come up with we have to talk with Hailey and see what she thinks," LaNae said.

"Hailey will probably agree with us. She's not that particular. I can't wait till we have to come up with a saying for that girl's T-shirt. I have hers all worked out in my head," Joy said.

"As I started to say before you both interrupted me..." Monique said jokingly rolling her eyes at LaNae and Joy. "...What about "The Last of the *Goode* Wives." And we should spell 'good' with an 'e' at the end."

"I like it! It's pretty direct and to the point. What do you think Joy?" LaNae said.

"Well...I like it too...but...it's too us," Joy said pointing at herself, LaNae, and Monique. "And I'm not sure if Shellie would be comfortable wearing that, especially with that 'e' on the end of good," Joy said really emphasizing the "d".

"She's not that uh...well you know what I mean. You and I would wear the heck out of a T-shirt with that saying, Monique. I'd have it put on a bright yellow shirt with black letters and the word "goode" in red italicized type. Let's think about it some more, but Monique, you're on the right track."

"What about '#1 Wife On Board'," LaNae suggested with a big smile.

"That one...I really like. It's simple but unique with the 'on board' at the end," Joy said happy to be able to stop brainstorming for ideas.

"Oh, let's get bold and put an 'A' in front of it so it reads: 'A#1 Wife On Board'. You said Shellie was strong when it came to handling conflict in her marriage," Monique said.

"I did say that, Monique, and Shellie is a very strong person. 'A#1 Wife On Board' says it all, girl! It's definitely direct. I think she'll like it a lot," Joy said.

"Well as soon we bounce the idea off Hailey, we can place the order this morning. Didn't you say we have to place it before noon in order to get the T-shirt back by two o'clock, Joy?" LaNae asked.

"That's right, LaNae. The guy was real sweet. I told him about our special day thing and explained that we would need a T-shirt made up each day for the next five days. He said he'd give us a ten percent discount and as long as we got our orders in on time he'd get the shirts back to us the same day. He said this was the best he could do for us. I told him we'd take whatever deal he could offer."

T-shirts were fifteen dollars apiece. The boutique had shirts in children and adult sizes (extra large, XX, and XXX too), and they came in a variety of colors. The wording was twenty-five cents a letter. Your name was free. The total cost for each T-shirt was not expected to exceed twenty-five dollars, and that was going to be split four ways. That meant each woman would be responsible for contributing to the cost of four shirts (excluding her own). It was inexpensive and everyone would have a souvenir T-shirt to take home.

"Has anyone thought about what color the T-shirt and lettering should be?" Monique asked.

"I think a lemon yellow shirt with some metallic silver-blue lettering would be classy. Why don't we get her one of those polo shirts instead of a T-shirt. She could wear it with pants or a skirt."

"I think that's a good idea, Joy," Monique said.

"Yeah, Shellie doesn't strike me as the T-shirt wearing type either," LaNae added.

"No, she isn't LaNae. She would probably wear it more if it were just a regular shirt."

"Well...I want a T-shirt, you guys. Don't go getting me anything dressy or classy," LaNae emphasized to her friends. "I'll be forty on Thursday and I want everyone on this ship to know about it. I'll be wearing my T-shirt all day long."

"All right, Ms. Feisty One. Be careful what you ask for because you might get it!" Monique said, winking at Joy.

The three women felt good about the saying they came up with for Shellie's T-shirt. They only hoped Hailey would go along with it and not have something else in mind.

Monique said she would get up first because she was hungry and wanted to eat an early breakfast in the dining room. She joked about whether there would be enough hot water left for Joy, let alone LaNae, to take a shower. Joy told Monique she'd better be in and out in five or she'd find her clothes floating in the ocean, and LaNae seconded that motion. Neither of the women meant it, but Monique got the point. She was out and dressed in twenty minutes and prepared to let them have the room to themselves. Joy and LaNae were going to do the aerobics thing before they ate breakfast.

Monique wasn't in the mood for a workout this early in the morning.

LaNae and Joy agreed to meet Monique back in the cabin around noon or twelve-thirty because by then they expected to be showered and changed after their workout. LaNae said she would definite be ready to eat lunch at that time.

Meanwhile...alone in her own cabin...Hailey turned over on her back to stretch. She slept heavy last night but she didn't feel completely rested this morning. *A good workout is what I need to get my blood moving*, she thought. It was about nine. Hailey recalled reading about the aerobics classes offered on the ship, but she wasn't sure about the times. She decided to get up anyway. If she got upstairs before the class started, she'd have a bagel with juice before her workout. She took a shower, tied her hair up in a ponytail, and put on a spandex exercise top and matching bicycle shorts. Her mid-section was flat and bare. The outfit was hot candy red. She looked good and felt good. Hailey was ready to work out, mainly so she could justifiably "pig out" at lunch.

Monique walked into the Caribbean Gem dining room fully prepared to fix a breakfast buffet plate and to eat it by herself when Shellie immediately called out to her. Monique didn't really want to eat with Shellie, but her actions would be completely misinterpreted if she did anything else. She smiled at Shellie and went over to sit down with her. She didn't have anything against Shellie. She just wasn't sure which direction their conversation would go, and she certainly didn't want to discuss husbands or family or the frustrations of being a wife on *her* cruise time. If Shellie wanted to talk about that sorta thing, she was going to have to find another listening ear. Monique made up her mind that she *would* excuse herself from the table if it became necessary.

"Hi, Shellie," Monique said.

"Hi, Monique. How is the cabin suite working out for all of you?"

"Actually...it's not too bad. I believe I left enough hot or should I say 'warm' water for LaNae and Joy to take their showers this morning. I was surprised about that."

"You're right, Monique. Hot or warm...water for a decent shower is a must."

"Our room stays at a comfortable temperature too."

"You're lucky. Last night, I had to sleep with an extra blanket. I don't sleep well if I'm cold."

"Me neither, Shellie, but I guess it wasn't that chilly in our room. It's tight quarters with the three of us in the same cabin, but we seem to be getting along pretty well. It's only been a day, though. We don't get the opportunity to hang out very often any more with LaNae living in Baltimore. So we'll appreciate this time together. I'm thinking we'll probably start to get on each other's nerves later in the week, but maybe not."

"Do you want to order something? Our waiter just left, but I'm sure he'll be back shortly."

"It's no problem, Shellie. I can wait till he comes back. I'm in no rush. I haven't made any plans this early in the day, unlike my two partners who 'planned' to do aerobics this morning before they ate."

"Workouts are good for your body, Monique. And, as slim as you look in that halter dress, are you trying tell me you don't work out?"

"No...I exercise, Shellie. More importantly, I watch what I eat. I break down and eat chips-n-dip and cookies and even pizza, but that's a once a month thing for me. I gotta fit my clothes, girlfriend."

"I know what you mean. I've never had a weight problem either. I not a big eater. I eat right, but I guess my family keeps me running," Shellie said.

Here we go, Monique thought. I hope she isn't going to start talking about that family of hers now. And when they were actually starting to have a decent and *enjoyable* conversation, the waiter soon came with Shellie's breakfast; and Monique ordered an omelette, bacon, juice, and dry toast. The subject did not return to families. Shellie and Monique continued to talk about health and fitness and even a little about NTW. Monique finally realized that she and Shellie had sat right across from each other in a business meeting about a month ago.

By the time Hailey got to the Main Deck lobby to look for the room across from the long winding bar, most of the passengers had assembled to begin the aerobics class. The instructor was kind of cute and quite muscular. Hailey just knew he was going work their butts literally *off*. She saw LaNae and Joy stretching and walked over to where they were standing.

"Morning ladies! Are we ready for this guy? Did you check out his BOD?"

"Yes we did...Hailey. He's supposed to look like that if he teaches aerobics for a living. Now isn't he?" Joy said, also admiring him standing in the front of the group. They were about two rows away from him.

"I just hope his class is good, and we sweat a little. This is the advanced class; if his routine is too complex, I won't be able to keep up. I hate being the only person out of step," LaNae said, checking out the men and women who all looked to be in pretty good shape. Some wore the flashier workout ensembles like Hailey. Others, like Joy, had a T-shirt and pair of sweat pants. LaNae wore warmup pants, a top, and tennis shoes.

"You won't be the only one out of step, LaNae. I'll be right behind you. I hope he doesn't go too fast either," Joy added.

Sidney introduced himself and welcomed the group to the advanced "Power Up" class. He explained that this class would meet every day at nine forty-five at this same location. He briefly mentioned that he also taught a senior "Active-n-Older" class at eight-thirty and an beginners/intermediate "Blast or Fast" class at three-fifteen. He asked everyone if they were ready to "burn some fat," and he politely told them they couldn't "snooze and loose!" (fat, that is) in *his* class. After getting the group pumped up and spirited, he said that today's session would be devoted to teaching them the exercise routine. He was going to start out at a slow pace so they could learn the steps. Tomorrow was show time. If they were brave enough to show up, they also had to keep up.

Sidney was a fitness expert with many years of experience. He taught the advanced group his five-part, fifty-minute exercise routine that allowed movement of all of the major muscle groups. He mixed the exercises up in his workouts. The first part consisted of conditioning exercises, including stretches and bends, but Sidney knew the advanced group came prepared, stretched, and ready to work out. Next, he had to teach them the steps for his moderate-impact aerobics routine that would warm them up. He interspersed this with an aerobics boxing routine that they liked a lot and easily grasped. The faster "jam crunch," a jogging and arm movement routine, took a little more time for the group to learn. Last, came Sidney's floor routine of tummy tighteners, leg shapers, hip trimmers, and the cool-down stretches. Overall, each part of the exercise routine lasted ten minutes when performed in sequence at Sidney's pace. By the time Sidney finished teaching them the steps, almost everyone in the class was sweating!

LaNae, Joy, and Hailey decided they didn't have the energy to walk back to their cabins and shower before they got a bite to eat. The workout was great! LaNae and Joy looked forward to tomorrow's class. Hailey said she'd have to think about coming back. *"I don't have enough fat for all of the routines he has us doing."*

About an hour later...

The air outside on deck kept their sweaty scents blowing downwind long enough for them to eat a bagel with water or juice. The three wanted a quick bite to hold them until lunch later that afternoon. The Sandy Beach Bar-n-Grill had bagels, cream cheese, and juices left over from this morning's buffet. A workout like that does something to your appetite. You definitely eat when your hungry, but you're appetite is satisfied after you eat and therefore, you don't need to snack between meals.

"Hailey, did Joy tell you we came up with a saying for Shellie's T-shirt?" LaNae asked after taking a sip of orange juice.

"That's right...today is Shellie's day. No, Joy didn't tell me. What did you come up with?"

"Well...how does 'A#1 Wife On Board' sound to you?" LaNae asked Hailey.

"That's a good one, guys! I don't know her too well, but I can't think of any reason why she wouldn't like it. She *is* a wife. I am too, but I have to tell ya that I wouldn't wear a shirt like THAT anywhere!" Hailey said. When she looked at Joy they both broke out laughing.

"I wouldn't either, Hailey, but for reasons quite different from yours, I'm sure." Joy said, still laughing with Hailey.

"I couldn't wear it either, Joy. I don't believe in false advertisement," LaNae said for reasons of her own that she too chose not to share at this time. She wondered where Solomon was and whether she would ever get the chance to meet with him secretly. She knew Joy and the other girls would eventually find out about him being on the ship. She was sorta prepared for the inevitable. On the other hand, she thought another day of him hiding out wouldn't be such a bad thing after all.

Hailey and LaNae went back to their cabins to shower and change. Hailey said she'd come over to their cabin after she was dressed. With Hailey's final okay on the wording, Joy decided she'd go to the T-shirt boutique and place the order first. The boutique opened at eleven. It was a few minutes after that. She told the owner what she wanted. She remembered that they had never really agreed on the style of shirt or the color of the lettering. She decided to let the owner give her some recommendations. He was the expert, not her. He suggested that she keep it simple with a basic white shirt and maybe gold or bright blue lettering. Joy said okay. Pickup was at two o'clock.

Joy's admirer caught a glimpse of her going into the T-shirt shop. He was a safe distance away, but he noticed her hair looked a little frayed and she was wearing sweat pants and a T-shirt. He wanted to speak to her but he knew the time was not right. Joy walked out of the shop. *It won't be as easy to watch her*, he thought. *I don't want to blow this!* After Joy left he went inside to talk with the owner.

When Solomon saw LaNae talking with Joy and Hailey as he stood outside on the Upper Deck looking down, it took everything in him not to walk down one deck, grab his woman, and passionately lay a kiss on her lips right in front of everybody. He had finally gotten the opportunity to see LaNae, albeit she was probably a little fatigued after her workout, he guessed, considering the clothes she had on. He decided he was coming out of hiding tonight. If not tonight, then it would definitely be sometime tomorrow.

Zeus, acting like a lion on the hunt, could barely concentrate on what he was supposed to do as Hailey walked past his bar. His radar eyes zoomed in on Hailey's hips in those red bicycle pants moving firmly from side to side. Zeus assumed she was going back to her cabin to change. Everything was tight on that girl. Nothing flabby back there, he thought. Sidney had apparently dismissed his advanced aerobics class. Hailey didn't see Zeus because he had just stood up after bending down to pull a bottle of wine from under the counter. He was setting the Emerald Palace Lounge up for the noon clientele. It was going to be another busy day. Zeus figured the opportunity to *squeeze that* would have to come later. He could tell she liked to party by the way she bounced when she walked. Zeus just wasn't sure if he was her type. All he knew was that she was *definitely his type*. He would get Sidney to check her out, though. He assumed she managed to survive the first day of his workout and that she was bound to be back tomorrow morning. Zeus couldn't wait to ask Sidney about her.

SIX

Tigers on the Prowl

About two hours later on the Caribbean Deck...

Not being able to talk to Joy was too much for the man on the prowl. He sat near the pool with a book laying face down in his lap. He had a towel thrown over his face and he was just about to take a nap because he hadn't been able to read the book. His thoughts wandered to the subject of having someone in your recent or previous past (and it didn't matter how much time had lapsed) who could still make your heart skip a beat. He considered it to be a magical moment to be in that person's space once again. He pondered about what type of person could have it that way with another person. Could he or she be a soul mate? A past lover? Or maybe just a very dear friend? He concluded that it really didn't matter. The best thing to do was to appreciate that person for the way they could make you feel.

❀

Hailey met up with LaNae and Joy in their cabin around twelve-thirty Monday afternoon. All three, having showered and freshened up, were dressed in bright colored, thin-strapped sun dresses and matching sandals. Hailey's dress was the only mini. It was royal blue. They decided to eat lunch in the Caribbean Gem dining room, which was on the ship's Middle Deck.

They all ached a little from their workout. Tomorrow would be the *real* test of how physically "fit" they were.

"Well...I ordered Shellie's shirt. I'll pick it up after we eat, and we can give it to her then," Joy said.

"I left a note on the bed for Monique. Wasn't she supposed to meet us before we left the room?" LaNae asked.

"Yes, she was. But it's okay. We need to talk about what we want to put on her shirt," Joy said.

"Yeah, that's right, Joy. Her day is tomorrow! Let's come up with something really wild for her," Hailey suggested.

"No, Hailey...really 'wild' is more appropriate for you!" Joy said jokingly.

"Maybe so, but we're not thinking about my shirt right now. And I don't care what you put on my T-shirt. I'm gonna wear it no matter what," Hailey said in rebuttal.

They got to the dining room and were seated. Arrangements had already been made for the five of them to sit together whenever they dined. The busboy who was assigned to their table for the duration of the cruise arrived immediately with a pitcher of water to fill the empty glasses on the table. After they reviewed the lunch menu, their waiter came to take their orders. He soon left and the three women continued their conversation.

"Hailey's got a point about Monique," LaNae said as she took a generous sip of her water. She was justifiably thirsty from this morning's workout. "You know Ms. Monique *can be* little on the wild side if she wants."

Joy went on to say: "True...but Ms. Monique is wild but also sophisticated so her T-shirt has to reflect pride and no nonsense."

"Can't we convey all of this and *still* have some fun with her?" Hailey asked.

"I believe we can, and I have a suggestion for a one liner," Joy said.

"Let's hear it, Joy. You usually have some good ideas," LaNae said.

"Well how does this sound: 'Yes, I'm Queen Bee, so stop *trippin'!*'" Joy said, waiting to hear their honest opinions. They were staring her right in the face.

"Well?" Joy repeated.

"Monique is gonna kill you, Joy, but *I like it!*" LaNae exclaimed.

"Girlfriend! That's a good one. I hope Monique knows we're just having fun with her," Hailey said.

"It's not too much, is it?" Joy said a little unsure now.

"No...it's Monique all right! That's what's so funny about it. She won't be able to deny who she really is with that written across her chest," LaNae said.

The waiter finally arrived with their lunch—club sandwiches and side salads. Joy had the soup de jour. LaNae ordered dessert.

"My guess is that Monique won't be able to deny ANYTHING. That T-shirt pretty much says it all. But girls, we don't want to hurt her feelings. You two know her better than me," Hailey said.

"We know her *quite* well, don't we, Joy? She'll just tell us to kiss her raggedy butt," LaNae said.

"Probably so," Joy added still feeling slightly appre-hensive. "But sometimes when the truth is presented to you it *can* hurt. Monique has feelings, in spite of her hard outer shell. She has a vulnerable side too, but don't either of you tell her I told you that."

"Why don't we see what Shellie thinks before we make any final decisions," Hailey suggested.

"That's a good idea, Hailey. I believe we all really like the wording, but one of us is just being a little worry wart," LaNae said, referring to Joy with a wide smile on her face.

"I have to admit the saying actually does convey how Monique feels about people in general," Joy said, clearly try-ing to rationalize the idea to herself.

"You know Monique will be okay with it. She knows that we would never do anything to hurt her. If she has a real problem, then she'll have to get over it. I won't hesitate to tell HER to stop trippin' if she goes there with me," LaNae said half-joking.

"I know you will, LaNae. The words capture the es-sence of Monique. I believe she'll be okay with it too. On the other hand, I'm not so sure she'll actually *wear* the T-shirt," Joy said.

"Well...she has to wear it. It's her special day, and we all agreed to do this," Hailey said.

"And that's what we'll tell her if she tries to pull rank and not wear her T-shirt, too," LaNae said, purposely sound-ing a little adamant.

"I'll let you two worry about how to get her to wear the darn thing. We'll get Shellie's input like Hailey suggested and then go from there," Joy said to close the subject to dis-cussion. It was perfect timing too. Monique was walking to-ward their table. She was wearing a bright red halter dress.

"Where have you been all morning and part of the afternoon?" Joy asked.

"Girl, I been around. I had breakfast with Shellie and then I went outside for a walk on the deck," Monique said as she sat down.

"Did you meet anyone? Or are you not scoping out the "lions and tigers and bears" on this cruise?" Joy asked.

"Are you referring to *men* when you use that phrase? Joy, you are so silly. Does everything you say have a connection to the Wizard of Oz?" Monique asked.

"I'm just an Oz fan. Calling men lions and tigers and bears doesn't mean anything specific. It's just my personal cliche, that's all," Joy said feeling offended by Monique's comment.

"Lions and tigers and bears! "Oh My!" Hailey uttered. "I think it's a cute way to refer to men. At least Joy is not male bashing. It's pretty innocent when you think about it."

Joy, still slightly ticked with Monique's criticism of her Oz fetish, changed the subject.

"Oh...Monique...we plan to give Shellie her shirt right after we leave here. Do you have plans to be somewhere this afternoon?"

"No...I guess I can hang out with you three for awhile. Maybe you can protect me from all those lions and tigers and bears on board our ship," Monique joked.

"Funny, Monique. Very funny," Joy said. "First, I have to pick the T-shirt up. Then I hope we can find Shellie. There are over a thousand passengers on board, you know."

"I left her sitting near the pool. It's on the Caribbean Deck, I believe. She was wearing a white coverup," Monique said.

"We'll we're just about finished, Monique," Hailey chimed in.

"Don't rush. Take your time eating. I haven't a care in the world right now," Monique said.

Little did she know, but her situation could change in the next day or two. Her "care in the world" was standing right outside the entrance to the dining room. Her back was facing him so he didn't see her *and* luckily she didn't see him.

"Let's all go now. We don't have a lot of time. While I pick up Shellie's shirt, why don't you three try to find her. We can meet on the Main Deck at the Emerald Palace Lounge. Let say in about fifteen minutes?" Joy said. It was one-thirty in the afternoon.

"Okay," Hailey said. LaNae and Monique nodded in agreement as they all got up from the table.

Sidney Masters pushed through the swinging doors to enter the room with the sign that read: "Cruise Employees Only." The staff were not allowed to eat with the passengers in the Caribbean Gem or the Garden of Eden dining rooms. Employees ate in a separate area adjacent to the front entrance of the Caribbean Gem. Seconds after Sidney walked through those swinging doors Monique and the others left.

Hailey, Monique, and LaNae walked out into the atrium of the Main Deck looking for Shellie. After Joy picked up the shirt, she went out on the Caribbean Deck to look for Shellie too. Joy remembered Monique saying she had left her sunbathing near the pool. When Joy got to the pool area there was no sign of Shellie. *She IS an adult woman*, Joy thought. *I'm not going to waste any more time worrying about where she is. If we can't find her, she'll get her shirt tomorrow*

along with Monique. It was in the mid-eighties and very humid outside. Joy was starting to perspire. She decided to go inside and see if the others had any luck. As she walked toward one of the ship's many entrances to the inside, she casually looked to the left then to the right. No one looked familiar. There were only parents preoccupied with their children and couples preoccupied with each other.

Hailey, Monique, and LaNae continued their search for Shellie. They walked through most of the small shops on the Main Deck. If Shellie was on another deck of the ship, then she was on her own, according to Monique. *She* wasn't looking all over the ship for an adult who perhaps didn't really want to be found. LaNae wanted to leave a message at the Information Desk for Shellie, but the other two women talked her out of that idea. If Shellie wasn't at the Emerald Palace Lounge then *"hey, we tried,"* was what Hailey was prepared to tell Joy if she asked. They continued to walk with the flow of people who seemed to be going in the same general direction toward the Emerald Palace Lounge.

There were many people on the ship. Not too many children. Monique was glad for that. Most of the passengers were dressed casually and were pretty laid back. Others, obviously more financially stable and very familiar with taking cruise vacations, walked and talked with an arrogance about them. Sometimes in different languages, too! The vibes from some of the richie rich (young and old) who walked past seemed to whisper *"You can't possibly afford this cruise!"* It almost made you feel like you were crashing *their* party. Some stared at you (or through you) and didn't say hello or even offer an acknowledging nod. And some gave you the "don't-even-think-about-coming-back" stare because you obviously forgot to pick that special invite card up on your way on board the first time. However, if you're not one to be intimidated, you raise your head high and walk like you and the ship's captain have been friends for a lifetime. You're supposed to be here because you are here.

When they got to the bar, Shellie was sitting on one of the barstools with about ten other people having a drink and talking to the bartender. He was cute, and Hailey couldn't wait for her introduction *and* a drink.

Shellie couldn't believe she was telling this young man everything about herself and her marriage. He introduced himself as "Zeus" and told her he'd been bartending since he was able to legally drink. She guessed he was a few years younger than her. However, he seemed to understand her, and he was also a good listener. His input from a man's perspective was helpful, and besides that she was intrigued by his personality. Shellie had ordered a martini. Before she finished the cocktail she could feel herself beginning to relax. Zeus knew his drink (slightly on the strong side) would do the trick. However, as they continued to converse about love and marriage, Zeus really didn't want to take advantage of Shellie. There was something genuinely honest and innocent about this woman. He liked talking to her, and the advice she gave him on women seemed sincere and truly from her heart. He didn't feel he was being judged by her. He felt like he could be himself. He was very comfortable with Shellie. No tricks or ulterior motives were necessary!

"Shellie, you're a hard person to track down," LaNae said talking with her hands on her hips.

"Oh…hi, girls. I'm sorry. I hope you weren't looking for me too long," Shellie said.

"You are grown, Shellie, and you don't need to check in with us. You paid for this cruise, and you can go wherever you want," Monique said prepared to defend Shellie.

"So who's your new friend?" Hailey asked. She had been watching Zeus since they walked over to the bar.

"Everyone...this is Zeus. He's been with this cruise line as head bartender off and on for about ten years."

"Not exactly. It's more like seven years with different cruise lines, and about three with this one. It seems like more than that," Zeus said.

"Well, meet Hailey, LaNae, and Monique," Shellie said, pointing to each one of them as she said their names. "Another friend is traveling with us named Joy."

"It's a pleasure to meet you all. Are you enjoying the cruise?" Zeus asked.

"It's been pretty good so far," LaNae said first. Monique and Hailey nodded in agreement. Hailey continued to watch him closely. Zeus, trying not to give her any special attention at this particular time, spoke generally to all three women.

"Can I get fix any of you ladies a drink?"

"What are you drinking, Shellie?" Hailey asked.

"A martini."

"Oh. I'll take a glass of wine, uh...did you say Zeus was your name?" Hailey inquired flirtatiously.

"Yes, that's right. Will that be white or red...and is that Mrs. or Ms.?"

"It's Mrs. since you asked. My first name is Hailey, remember? And make that white wine, please."

"Okay Mrs. Hailey, white wine coming up."

"Anything for you two ladies? Last call for the minute."

"No. Too early for me," LaNae said.

"Sorry, I don't drink this early either," Monique added.

"That's fine. But let me know if you change your mind."

He left to fix Hailey's drink.

"He is so cute," Hailey said.

"Yes he is," Shellie added. "We've been talking for about twenty minutes. He's been quite the gentleman."

"I'd like to get to know how gentle of a man he really is," Hailey said.

"I'll bet you would," LaNae said.

"He seems young though," Hailey said.

"He's probably your age, Hailey," Monique commented.

"You think so?"

"Yes, Hailey. I'm in my late thirties. He's probably in his early thirties. Aren't you?" Shellie asked.

"Yes, I'm thirty-three, Shellie."

"Well Hailey you'll have plenty of time to get to know him *and* to spend your money all at the same time," Monique said, knowing Ms. Hot Pants couldn't wait to be alone with the man.

"I'm not that interested in him. I just think he's cute."

"Okay, Hailey. You don't need to explain your business to us," Monique smiled.

Zeus returned with Hailey's wine. He laid a cruise ship cocktail napkin on the counter, upon which he placed a tall slender stemmed glass of wine. A narrow strip of blue ribbon was daintily wound around the entire stem of the glass. The blue even matched Hailey's dress. Hailey was surprised. Zeus had wanted to impress this lady. He succeeded.

"Thank you," she smiled and nodded.

"That was *very* creative of you, Zeus," Shellie said.

LaNae and Monique didn't think his simple gesture was *that* impressive.

Then Joy approached everyone sitting at the bar.

"Well I'm glad we all managed to find our way back together again," Joy said.

"Joy, I want you to meet someone," Shellie said.

"Who?"

"Our bartender friend. His name is Zeus."

"Pleased to meet you," Joy said extending her hand to shake his.

"My pleasure...and your name is?"

"It's Joy Sharpe."

"A beautiful name. And you wear it well," Zeus replied. He was going to be a little smoother with this one.

"Thank you, uh...Zeus. You have a captive audience of women. I guess you wear your name well too," Joy said.

"No, I just like my job and for people to have a good time."

"I just bet you do."

Joy turned her attention to her girlfriends. "I guess we could give the shirt to Shellie right here if you want. What do you guys wanna do?"

"Yeah, why not, Joy," Monique said.

"Let me give it to her!" Hailey offered as she finished drinking her glass of wine.

"Okay, Hailey here's the shirt," Joy said as she handed her the small merchandise bag labeled 'Mr. T's-Shirt' to Hailey. Joy sat down on the empty barstool next to Shellie.

Hailey stood up as if she were giving a prepared address to the nation and said: "Shellie, most of us don't know you too well, but I think I speak for everyone—except Joy—in saying that we can't wait to get to know you better." Hailey handed Shellie the bag and walked back to her barstool. She could have been nervous from her one-liner speech or slightly tipsey from that glass of wine she consumed so quickly. No one really knows. All everyone does know is that watching her *miss* the barstool and end up on floor was about the most hilarious thing they had ever seen. And with that mini dress on too? Well let's just say that *how she fell* was more of mystery than how her *stuff looked* with her legs up in the air. LaNae and Monique jumped off their stools to help Hailey.

They fought harder to stifle their laughter, but when Hailey stood up to pull her dress down and *she* was laughing out of embarrassment, they lost the battle and fell out themselves. Luckily, it happened so quickly that the incident didn't draw too much attention. (Hailey wasn't on the floor for more than two seconds!) Most people who walked past them just saw everyone laughing. Zeus missed seeing her fall from his side of the bar. However, he did see her pulling down that mini-dress. And he would probably swear that he saw something else that he shouldn't have seen...and that's with his left hand resting on a *stack* of Bibles and his right hand raised to the heavens!

After everyone was able to recover gracefully from the falling of Hailey's comet (once again), Shellie was able to open her gift. She was even a little teary eyed when she read the inscription on the shirt. We didn't ask whether it was because *we* surprised her or Hailey's surprise falling. She said she'd wear her T-shirt proudly. *"It really reflects how I feel as a wife,"* were her exact words. Monique closed her eyes discreetly and *prayed* Shellie wouldn't dwell on that very topic. Monique wasn't in the mood to talk about the trials of being a wife, a parent—or being married, for that matter. Everyone had trials. She was enduring hers, and she expected no less from anyone else. There simply was no free ride in any relationship. It was supposed to be a *lifetime commitment* with all the ups and downs, that is, unless someone made a decision not to stick it out.

seven
Hide and Seek Out

The five women

stayed at the Emerald Palace Lounge talking with Zeus for another hour or so. It was close to three in the afternoon before they even thought about leaving. Zeus was a cool guy, and he kept them laughing with many interesting and funny cruise stories. LaNae, Joy, and Hailey mentioned their workout early that morning. Hailey told him how that fitness instructor made them do a *gazillion* exercises, but that his routines were creative and hip. Zeus was proud to tell them that he grew up with the very-popular-back-then-and-now "Sidney Masters." Monique switched barstools with Joy, and she and Shellie moved to the other end of the bar to continue the private conversation they started earlier that morning. (This was at Shellie's request and *against* Monique's better judgment.) Therefore, Monique never *actually heard* Zeus say Sidney's name. It was best that she didn't.

Anyway…Zeus went on to tell them how he had front row seats to the most hysterical exercise sideshow at eight-thirty in the morning. Sidney's seniors aerobic class for passengers who were fifty-five and up was a hoot! These older adults did their bends and squats all right, but some also moaned and groaned, according to Zeus. The one or two women who wanted *extra* help from Sidney during the workout were the funniest! Zeus told them how Sidney had mentioned a particular woman named Janeen McClaine. Janeen wanted Sidney so badly according to what Sidney told Zeus that she was willing to pay the cruise line top dollar to hire Sidney to *aerobicize her* from top to bottom. It didn't matter because Sidney would never take Janeen up on her offer. He couldn't justify giving up his unlimited access to single *and married* women to tend to one old wrinkled up and probably used one.

Women like Janeen (and men too!) will never be able to make the best of their long-time marriages as long as they continue to look for "outlets" for their passionless relationships. These outlets can be any age, shape, size, or race. These elder pleasure seekers have gone so long without passion in their thirty- and forty-year-plus relationships that they almost *have* to look for outlets. Some men use the outlets to see if they still have a bit of lion, tiger, and bear in them, and some women want to fill the void in their life, specifically that emotional one resulting from *no* physical attention. A couple in this predicament will never experience true happiness together so they end up in a rut. They have to make a conscious effort to put some zest in their uneventful life. Over the years the basic things that used to make both partners click and respond fondly to one another may be forgotten. This happens to couples young and old. And what's worse is that no one wants to talk about it. Ultimately, the two end up living like roommates. The give and take in any relationship has to be balanced out with some real compassionate love in order to survive in today's world. There are just too many distractions, if you know what I mean.

Meanwhile at the other end of the bar, Shellie and Monique shared opinions on how best to balance out the giving and taking in each of their respective marriages. Shellie told Monique how she and her husband were at a standstill given his recent news about being gay and having a lover. Monique *definitely* wasn't ready to hear that. She did manage to hide her dismay. Shellie asked Monique if their conversation could be kept private. She said she wasn't ready to share the latest happenings in her life with Joy at this point. Monique agreed. Shellie also told Monique that she came on this cruise to think about whether she wanted to stay in her marriage. Monique was slightly confused. *Hadn't this White woman just told her that her husband had an affair with a MAN?* What was Shellie so indecisive about? The situation had a quick fix in Monique's opinion. HE HAD TO GO! It was plain and simple to Monique that the marriage was over. She listened to what Shellie had to say out of sheer curiosity. How and why certain people stay in their marriages during what appears to be the worst of times is truly a mystery.

"I still love him, I guess. I also have my children to think about," Shellie said.

"Those are valid concerns, Shellie," Monique said.

"But...can a person just stop being gay? He didn't exactly say he wanted to be with this 'Robin' person," Shellie said quietly.

"Did he say he wanted to be with you and the kids?"

"No...he didn't say that either."

"So why do you think he wants to stay married to you?"

"Because he didn't say he wanted to end our marriage. I just told him I needed some time to decide whether *I* wanted to stay."

"Oh…that's a little different. But did your husband say he loved this other man?"

"No. We didn't really talk about him *or* them. He just told me he had the affair. I'm not sure whether this man is still in his life or not."

"O-KAY…let's assume he's not. How do you feel about the fact that your husband has been with another man?" Monique couldn't wait to hear Shellie's answer to her question. She knew how she felt about it. If her hubby wanted to experience how it felt for a man to rock his world then there would never be an opportunity for him to *re-experience her stuff* again. He'd have to lay in *that* man's bed for the rest of his life or find another woman who'd have to take her chances with him and that AIDS bug.

"I guess I was a little more outraged about him having an affair with a man than I was about him having an affair *period*. But I feel like I need to give him a second chance because he gave me one," Shellie said. She went on to tell Monique how she got involved with a man and that her husband found out. He left the house for a few weeks, but he did return. They talked about it (not in great detail); and, as the years went by, their relationship got better. Shellie knew something wasn't right a few years after that because her husband started to change and later he just stopped being intimate with her. They still slept together but he was on the left side and she laid on the right side of their king sized bed. Then one day a few months ago he decided to tell her about his lover. She had no warning. He came in late one night and just told her.

"Well if you give him this second chance you think he deserves, how can you be sure he won't see his lover again?"

Monique asked still in awe of Shellie's dedication and commitment to her marriage.

"I can't be. Trust in the Lord is all I have. Should be all I need. Funny I don't feel that way," Shellie said.

"I know. But we should. The Man upstairs is really all the man we need in our lives. Easy to say...not so easy to put in practice when you're lonely," Monique admitted.

"Yeah...lonely is exactly how I feel right now," Shellie said.

"You shouldn't feel that way, Shellie. You have Joy in your corner and you know how supportive she is. I'm here for you too. I can't help you decide what to do though. Giving it to the Lord is the right thing to do. Let the peace of mind he ultimately blesses you with direct your heart and help make your decision. The Lord has an answer for most of the difficult decisions we have to make in life. My Grandmother Dee once told me that he whispers the right message to us. All we have to do is listen with a compassionate heart and prayerful mind, then our decision is Gospel, and therefore usually the right one."

"I believe that whatever my decision will be I'm going to make sure I have my peace of mind. It's the only way I can live with it. I do have my children to think about though," Shellie said.

"Now if you are happy then your children will be happy. The reverse is true too," Monique reminded her.

"I have to agree with you, Monique. They already suspect something is wrong because I decided to take this cruise alone. We always take trips together. This solo act is probably very confusing to them. But I was very desperate to get away so I could think about my life and what direction I wanted to go."

"You do have a difficult decision to make and I'm sorry this cruise isn't a pleasure trip."

"Well I don't plan to be depressed about my marriage the entire cruise! I'm going to dress up for dinner tonight, and I even plan on going to that midnight buffet I heard they have on these cruises, if I can stay awake."

"You go, girl. Don't think about your decision for the next few days. You have five days left, and you should really make the most of them. We'll be stopping at our first port of call tomorrow some time. We can all get off this ship and take a stroll on the beach."

"I can't wait for this ship to dock. But on a more serious note, Monique, you have been a good friend to me and we just met, too. I appreciate you giving me so much advice. Sorry we didn't get to talk about you. Are you having any problems in your marriage?"

"We don't want to go there, girl. I'm just hanging in there and trying to remain civil with my man. It's not a perfect marriage if there is such a thing. The passion is a little weak but he takes care of his business at home. I don't have much to complain about. I guess I still love him, too."

"Sounds like you continue to work through your problems and that's good. Keep the communication lines open, Monique. If you don't, your problems will escalate," Shellie said.

"You're right, Shellie. Let's move down to see what those three are talking about now. I'm glad that Hailey has Joy and LaNae to chaperone her butt. Talk about being boy crazy. That girl seems a little desperate to me."

"She's just having fun. She's married, you know," Shellie said.

"And...is that supposed to mean something?"

"It should."

"I think it should too, but Hailey has another opinion on the subject. I'm willing to bet on that," Monique smiled.

Monique and Shellie moved back down to where the other women were sitting, and might I add laughing and drinking. Both Joy and LaNae had half-filled glasses sitting in front of them. Zeus was a real charmer.

About fifteen minutes later the women decided to check out the scenery on the other decks. They hadn't visited the gynasium and spa on the Mediterranean Deck, the all night dance club on the Red Sea Deck, nor the sunroof on Upper Deck. They promised Zeus they would return for laughs and conversation with him before the end of the cruise. Hailey made a personal promise to herself that she'd be seeing him again too, but much sooner than the others.

Just as Monique stood to leave with the others, Sidney, still quite a distance away, was walking toward her. She didn't see him. He, however, *did* recognize her. He slowed up his pace. He had to tell Howard about this! Luckily, Monique was walking in the opposite direction and never looked backed as he approached the bar. Sidney was dressed and prepared for his three-fifteen workout class, beginners and intermediates together. He was *not* prepared for this woman to be on his cruise ship! He panicked. He could hardly breathe. Hadn't he shared with Howard his instinctive feelings that this woman was close, somehow nearby? And as for the women she seemed to be traveling with? Weren't they in his morning exercise class? Yes, they were. The White woman looked good in those red bicycle shorts, but she complained too much. The other one had on sweat pants. She seemed to enjoy the workout routines. *What am I going to do now? What if this woman decides to work out with her friends tomorrow? I won't be able hide from her then.* He couldn't believe it was the woman he'd met in New York. He wasn't exactly sure why he was so apprehensive about seeing her again. They just had a good time together. He didn't have her number or address because they hadn't planned to keep in touch. What *was* the big to-do. Sidney had to think hard and *fast*. He had about ten minutes before his class began. He needed to slow his racing heart down, first. His palms were sweaty, but his breathing was getting more normal. He knew exactly what it was. This woman *affected him* like no other woman had ever done. He wasn't in love with her or anything. He was just moved emotionally (not sexually) whenever he thought about her. He never figured he'd *ever see* her again! She gave him the warmest, most comfortable feeling inside. She had a calming spirit about her. He, on the other hand, had goosebumps and felt dizzy like a senior going on his first date to the prom. This was not good! Sidney was no school boy! He had most things in his life under control. This sista was messin' him UP!

"Howie! Who were those women?" Sidney asked, his voice shaking slightly.

"Relax, man. They're just some women I met. We only talked for about an hour. What's the problem?"

"What about the one in the halter dress?"

"What about her? I can't remember her name. It's Monica or Maria?" Howard was trying to remember.

"No...I think it's Monique or something. I can't remember her last name. Anyway what did she talk to you about?"

"I didn't really talk to her. She was talking with Shellie."

"Who's Shellie?"

"This really nice White woman I met. We talked for awhile before her friends came over looking for her. Then Shellie was talking to...what did you say her name was?"

"Monique, Howard."

"Yeah, come to think about it...it was Monique. Anyway...Monique and Shellie talked alone at the other end of the bar. I guess it was private. I didn't hear their conversation. I was having a pretty good time with the other three women, though. Sid, why are you asking me all these questions anyway?"

"Because the women in the red dress is the ONE!"

"The ONE...what?" Howard asked sounding a little irritated because he really didn't know what Sidney was talking about.

"The woman I told you about this morning. You know. I told you I was thinking about her and felt strange about it."

"You mean to tell me she's right here on this ship?"

"Yeah, Howie. Didn't I say I had a feeling she was close?"

"You sure did, man. What are you going to do now?"

"I know what I'm *not* going to do."

"And what's that?" Howard anxiously asked.

"I'm not going to let her know I'm on board this ship so I don't want her to see me. At least not now. She makes me too nervous."

"This is weird, Sidney. It's not like you to hide from a woman."

"Howard, you don't know the affect this woman has on me." Sidney kept turning around on his barstool as if he expected Monique to sneak up on him.

"I guess not, man."

"Well do you think she saw you? She may not even recognize you, Sid."

"I not taking *any* chances. I'm not ready for her, so don't mention my name, okay?"

"Too late, man." Howard laughed.

"Wudda mean, Howard? Did you mention my name to her?"

"No, her friends are in your morning workout class. They were talking about it so I just told them your name.

That's it. They probably won't remember it. This Monique person probably didn't hear me cause she was sitting farther down the bar. She didn't act like she heard."

"Well, don't talk about me anymore, and don't mention my name, man."

"Okay, don't worry about me saying anything. What if she happens to recognize you?"

"I told you what she does to me, Howard. I can't go out like that, man. I got my pride, you know. I just need to understand what it is she does to me and be able to handle it. Then I'll be all right."

"You said there was nothing between you two, right?"

"Yeah, that's right. And I plan to keep it that way too."

"You do what you have to do, Sidney. You know I'll cover for you if I have to."

"Thanks, man. I have to go. My class is waitin' for me. I can see them from here. Thanks again Howard."

"You got it that way with me, man. I'll look out for her and try to warn you if she's coming in your direction."

"Great man, thanks. I gotta go. I'm late now." Sidney said as he trotted across the lobby to the recreation room.

Everyone was dressed for dinner at eight. They were dining in the Garden of Eden tonight. Even Hailey was on time. All five were sitting together. Water glasses were filled by their busboy and menus were provided by their waiter. The selection of food was quite impressive. To start off there were appetizers consisting of smoked Pacific salmon, Tequila shrimp, baked brie, and shrimp or fruit cocktail. The soups included corn and crabmeat chowder, wild game consomme, and the soup of the day. They had three kinds of salad from which to choose, namely, mixed green, spinach and tomato, and heart of lettuce. And the entrees were wonderfully prepared as well. There was duckling, lamb, pheasant, veal, filet mignon, or chicken. No one ordered the cheese and cracker tray. The desserts were equally tantalizing. Strawberry shortcake, chocolate mousse, baked alaska, and almond-flavored parfait, not to mention the assortment of ice cream in many flavors. The women agreed they could easily get used to fine dining like this for the next five days.

The menu changed daily, and Joy said she'd be the adventurous one and have a different entree every night. LaNae said she could be adventurous too, but only with the dessert menu, and Hailey said she would have a different cocktail drink every night. They all knew with whom.

They got through dinner all right. LaNae excused herself after they had eaten, saying she wanted to take an early evening stroll alone on the Upper Deck to look at the moon and stars. When Monique left to go to the ladies' room, Joy seized the opportunity to tell Shellie what they wanted to have inscribed on Monique's T-shirt. Shellie thought the words were more than appropriate for Monique, although she didn't exactly know what the word *"trippin'"* meant. She asked Joy, who told her it means overreacting to or getting upset about something someone else thinks is unimportant or insignificant. Shellie sorta understood after that.

LaNae found a secluded spot on the Upper Deck. She was hoping Solomon might have come up here to think. No one he knew would be up here. As LaNae looked out at the glistening water and felt a slight breeze blowing, two hands encircled her waist. She said it in a low voice but loud enough for whomever had their hands around her to hear: "This better be you, Solomon." *And it was!*

eight

Monique's Moment

"I wasn't sure if I was *ever* going to see you on this ship, LaNae," Solomon said.

"I know, Solomon. I'm not so sure this was a good idea."

"Well it's a little late now. I'm here, aren't I?" Solomon grabbed LaNae's hand when he said this.

"Yes, you are. And I'm really glad," LaNae said not as enthusiastic as Solomon had expected.

"So why so anti-climatic?" he asked.

"Because I don't want anyone to know about us, yet," LaNae didn't want to tell him how *afraid* she was of someone finding out.

"Why not? We're just close friends, LaNae. There's nothing else to it."

"But we can't even *let* people know we're just friends, as you say. I don't like having to deny how important your friendship is to me," she said sadly.

"But we have to, LaNae. Otherwise, people will draw conclusions about us. And we can't do anything about what people think or say. Rumors would get out. Are you ready to deal with that crap?" Solomon asked.

"No. So how long do we keep the secrets and lies going?" LaNae asked.

"Well, just what do you want the world to know?" Solomon smiled.

"I want to tell the world that you're my loving friend, and there isn't a thing I wouldn't do for you on this earth." LaNae was very specific.

"So, LaNae, if you love me why don't you tell the world. Just shout it out. I want the world to hear it right now." Solomon wanted to hear it as well. He was quite honest about his feelings for LaNae.

"Okay...Hey W-O-R-L-D! Guess what? I'm in *LOVE* with Solomon E. Moore!" LaNae yelled out over the whipping ocean waves. There was no reply.

"Feel better?"

"A little. But I still don't like having to deny what's real about us."

"Me neither, but..." she cut Solomon off in mid-sentence.

"Both of us still have a bit of reality waiting for us at home. You haven't forgot have you? What are we going to do about them? Continue to deny their existence?" LaNae was determined to get an answer from him on every question.

"No, I guess neither of us can do that for very long," Solomon said.

"Okay, so *what are we going to do*?" LaNae needed some answers. They had issues to resolve, and she wasn't letting him off the hook.

"I'm not sure."

"Then why did you decide to come on this cruise?"

"Because you asked me. And...how could I say no to you?"

"Do you expect to spend much time with me? You know when Joy finds out you're on this ship, she's going to freak. And trust me Joy *will* find out. Monique, too, but she won't care either way."

"We'll have to deal with that when we have to, 'L'," Solomon said wanting to avoid any discussions about the inevitable.

This was a first, LaNae thought. He has never called me *"L."* What have I gotten myself into once again. Hadn't I walked down this path years ago? I had this man not only out of my life but out of my system at one point. I obviously didn't learn my lesson then. Perhaps I'm *supposed* to now. I know how I feel about Solomon and also how he feels about me. It seems legal as long as we don't have sex, I think. How strong are our feelings for each other? Will we eventually give into those intimate desires we've managed to suppress for so long? I guess at that point sex would be a last resort out of pure desperation. I sometimes wonder if Solomon is always going to be a part of my life...and own a piece of my heart. All I really know is that I can't seem to escape from him. It's like he and I have a friendship plus bond that has *never* threatened either of our commitments to remain married...until now.

Married men like Solomon are able to justify keeping "the other woman" in their lives, because it's easier than making the decision to give up the security of the wife and family. But for most married women, keeping that "other man" in *their* lives, especially if they have kids, is too darn emotional. And it never seems to work out favorably for the woman. That's how LaNae felt about it anyway. She wasn't going to keep this juggling act up for the rest of her life. Solomon was going to be either IN or OUT. And she would have the deciding vote on this. For some reason now that he was here. She was not leaning so much toward that "IN" side.

I can almost accept his love for me and my love for him without feeling like I have to have an "us" to make me complete and happy, she thought. *It takes too much energy to tend to us and my personal life at home. I can't do it anymore. And I won't. It's a disservice to my husband and something that will just age me in the long run.*

Solomon and LaNae both stood quite close to each other against the rails on the Upper Deck enjoying the romantic setting, the breeze, and the rushing sound of the water as the ship parted the seas. They reminisced about some silly times, and pondered what their next move would be as far as spending time together during the rest of the cruise. Solomon suggested they meet here every other night. They should also definitely take a walk together on the beach in Cancun. Solomon said he'd find LaNae or leave a message for her at the ship's information desk on the day they docked specifying a meeting place and time.

Solomon and I are going to be just luvin' buddies, LaNae thought. What was wrong with that? Joy would say a whole lot was wrong. She wouldn't approve of any married women's involvement with a lion, tiger or bear type of man. Who else could judge her justifiably on her relationship with Solomon? She knew exactly who and what Book He would be using. She knew it all to well.

Shellie just barely woke up in time. She went back to her cabin early, actually right after one performance by the live band that played for a few hours during their dinner. Joy went to her cabin at midnight after she and the others had hung out for a while. *Hanging out* consisted of a visit to the ship's casino, a *re-visit* to Emerald Palace Lounge at Hailey's request, and then a trip upstairs to check out the dance floor in the OZ Club at Monique's request. No one was out *on their good foot* dancing that night, at least no one Monique wanted to see.

When Shellie finally got dressed to join them, they followed the crowd to the late night buffet in the Garden of Eden. It was a spectacular sight! The buffet started at one in the wee morning and many people were lined up to fill their plates. The buffet line was the chef's exquisite layout of sliced meats, vegetables, fruits, and finger foods (no chicken wings or fried mozzarella cheese sticks, O-kay?) and lots of DES-SERTS! The elegant arrangement of the trays of appetizers, cakes, pies, and pastries was a true work of art. And this was a nightly event!

A huge twelve-foot mold of The Lady of the Sea (during King Arthur's time) was intricately carved out of a block of ice and positioned at the front entrance to the dining room. The theme of the room's decor was the ocean and the deep blue sea. Beautiful ice sculptures of penguins, dolphins, seagulls, and a fisherman, as well as every type of snail, fish, or sea creature imaginable, were placed on the buffet line or located somewhere in the dining room for all eyes to see and revere.

Joy and the others had no idea that this was what cruising was all about. "I still can't believe we're on this cruise together!" Joy said.

"Well...we are, Joy," LaNae replied.

"Now please don't start boo-hooing again," Monique jokingly pleaded. Earlier that day, Joy had barely gotten through dinner without shedding a few tears. She got emotional about everything.

"I won't Monique, so you don't have to worry," Joy said as she quickly wiped the corner of her left eye with a single finger.

After everyone had impressively full plates in their hands, the five found a table and *thoroughly grubbed down*. They stayed up until two-thirty that morning!

As he laid in his cabin bed, around two in the morning, he was thinking again. He decided to never watch Joy again unless he was far enough away and surrounded by people to allow him to blend in with the crowd. That was safe way to operate. And he was a smooth operator. He had his three C's in order now, his confidence, his control, and his Cool. He was always ready for most things that happened during his lifetime, except for two things. He *wasn't* ready to lose his parents and he *wasn't* ready to lose his high school girlfriend of seventeen months. However, he *was* ready to see and talk with Joy. He hadn't exactly figured out when or how, though.

It dawned on him this early morning that there were similarities between Joy and that old girlfriend of his. She and Joy looked alike, talked alike, and more than that they acted alike. His old girlfriend's personality was serious and playful, so much like Joy's that the stranger was shocked the first time he actually laid eyes on Joy. Another similar trait of both women was that they took care of business. He mostly liked that trait of the two women. It was still very hard to comprehend and accept their similarities, no less. He was going to let her know he was on the ship in some way. *"Think,"* he said quietly to himself. *"I know!"* He said it out loud. *"I could do it at this Captain's Cocktail Party on Thursday."* He decided he was going walk up to Joy and ask her to dance with him. Yes, he was going to make his move then. He'd be dressed to kill. He smiled. He was thinking long and hard about how perfect the evening would be and how wonderful it would be to finally have his arms around his Joy.

Tuesday morning...

Sidney woke up feeling tense. He was worried about his advanced class and just who might be in attendance. That little talk he had with Howard yesterday hadn't really eased his mind, nor was he completely focused during his beginners/intermediate workout class. However, he knew he could conduct this class with his eyes closed. He was practically doing it now. His mind was definitely preoccupied with this Monique woman. *What if she shows up at my workout this morning? I could play her off and act like I don't know her. But that would be downright rude and wimpy on my part. I'm just going to have to face this head on. I can handle this girl! She's not my woman...and I'm not her man. So why am I so nervous about seeing her?*

It was another fun day at sea. The passengers were getting comfortable about going from one deck to another. *Serenade the Seas* was becoming everyone's vacation home away from home. Where you dined for meals was dependent on what you wanted to eat and how you wanted to dress. There were myriad options for food, drinks, and entertainment. The weather was suburb for vacationing, and there were four more days of crusin' left! If you're fortunate enough to cruise with a partner then you know romance is in the air both day and night. You really can't knock a vacation like this. Everyone should take a cruise at least once.

LaNae and Joy were definitely doing aerobics after last night's "pig out." Monique said she'd pass on it this time. *"Maybe tomorrow,"* she said. They knew Shellie was still asleep. Hailey said she'd be there if she woke up in the mood to move her body in a *gazillion* ways again. (That girl was wearing that word out!) She asked LaNae and Joy to go without her. That way she wouldn't feel guilty if she decided not to go at the last minute. Joy also wanted to order Monique's T-shirt. She planned to make a stop at Mr. T's-Shirt on the way. Most of the boutiques were located on the Main Deck, including Sidney's workout classes. It was going to be a *Monique* (as opposed to unique) *moment* when Ms. Handle It got her T-shirt today! (And maybe more than that if Sidney decided to come correct enough to show his face to her.)

Sidney's workout was about to get under way. He had already begun to sweat, in the palms of his hands, that is. He wasn't sure what he would do if Monique showed up this morning. He only hoped if she *did* that he could still do his job. He wasn't about to let her see him "sweat" in any capacity except during or after a good workout. Sidney needed to burn off some of his nervous energy. He was going to work this group hard today. They'd be able to keep up. He was almost certain about that. *"Well...let's get this show on the road,"* he said to himself. Monique's three friends had already arrived without her. He was even surprised to see Hailey, who had complained so much after the first day. Sidney took a deep breath and moved out to the front of the room to do what he did best.

"O-KAY! Sidney's In The House...Let's Pump It Up...Pump It UP! Sidney shouted. And the class responded loudly with: "Pump It Up...Pump It UP!" All you could hear after that was the music, mostly the beat of the base guitar, and the class counting one-two-three.

The workout was a little more than they expected. LaNae and Joy assumed the aching-n-paining would have reared its ugly head by now. They had a little soreness in their legs and arms, but not much. Perhaps they were fit after all!

Sandy Beach on Middle Deck was the late lunch spot for the five women this afternoon. Shellie eventually wandered out on deck to join them. She had eaten a light breakfast but she wasn't hungry. Joy thought after lunch would be the perfect time to give Monique her T-shirt. It was just a little before noon in the afternoon. The weather was perfect. They sat at a table with a huge umbrella that effectively kept the bright sun rays off of them.

"Who's got an introductory speech for Monique before we give her what she's been waiting to get for the past two days at sea. And Hailey because you already spoke for Shellie, let's have someone else do it for Monique, all right?" Joy said.

"Oh...that's no problem, Joy," Hailey nodded.

"I'd like to say something, Joy," Shellie said as she smiled at Monique.

"Go right ahead, girlfriend," Joy said encouragingly. Shellie turned her chair a little to face Monique.

"Monique, I've had the pleasure of getting to know you better for the past two days. It has truly been an honor. You are such a self-assured and take-charge woman. I respect you for that, and when others read your T-shirt, they'll respect you as well." Then Shellie handed the boutique bag to Monique. When Shellie finished they all applauded. They tried hard to hide their grins. You *know* they wanted to scream.

"What did you guys do? This T-shirt...I don't know if I wanna open this bag. Joy, I know you came up with this one on your own to get me back. Remember, payback can and will be on YOU on Friday," Monique said. She was just a tiny bit apprehensive about peeking inside the bag.

"Just open it, Monique!" everyone yelled.

Monique opened the bag and with a half-smile on her face pulled the T-shirt out and read the inscription: "Yes, I'm Queen Bee, so stop *trippin'!*" The boutique owner had really jazzed Monique's shirt up. The shirt was aqua blue with white lettering. The letters in the word "trippin'" were slanted. Monique's mouth fell wide open.

"What are you guys trying to say about me? I can't wear this anywhere. People will think I'M the one who's TRIPPIN'," she laughed. "I like it 'cause it's the truth! But I don't know if I'm brave enough to wear it."

"You have to wear it, Monique," Hailey said. The others said the same thing.

"People will be talking about me behind my back. I don't know, you guys. I have to think about this one."

"Oh Monique, loosen up. It's just for fun. Half the people don't even know what the word trippin' means," Joy said, hoping Shellie wouldn't be offended in the slightest way.

"Yes, they will. You can tell from the context. Anyway, it's the words "Queen Bee" that really have me worried. Don't get me wrong, you guys. I like the shirt and it's definitely me, but we're on a ship. There are people everywhere! I just wouldn't be comfortable wearing it on the ship. I'll wear it when we go ashore, though. I won't look familiar to anyone there. Thank you! All of you,...I really love it," Monique said sincerely.

"All right, Monique. You know you're chumping out on us. But we'll go along with you because it's your special day," Joy said.

"Go on and wear that T-shirt, Monique. No one will care what it says. This is a cruise. Everyone's doing a little bit of this and little bit of that," LaNae said, and she suddenly realized how true that statement was for her when it came to Solomon being on the ship.

"Yeah, Monique. You gotta wear it sometime today to make your day official," Hailey begged.

"All right, I'll wear it for lunch since we're out here," Monique said as she took her top off and slipped the T-shirt over her head. She had a black swim suit on underneath her shorts and top. She was planning to do the Jacuzzi thing later on. She told them she'd wear the shirt until then.

"I sure hope no one's watching me," Monique said as she quickly pulled her top off.

Well Sidney couldn't help but watch her. He was sitting at another umbrella table on deck. He was *so busy* watching, in fact, that he nearly choked on the burger he was wolfing down. He wanted to grab a bite to eat before his three-fifteen class. From where Sidney was sitting he couldn't actually read the shirt's inscription. However, when he got up to leave he was discreetly close enough to read it; he made no attempt to hide his broad smile.

Hailey decided she was going back to her cabin to change out of her exercise gear. She admitted that today's workout wasn't so bad after all. When Monique left, LaNae, Joy, and Shellie did some light talking. Shellie asked if they had any ideas on what they were going to put on Hailey's shirt. LaNae said, whatever they did, it was going to be wild because Hailey wouldn't want it any other way. Joy, who knew Hailey best, agreed wholeheartedly. Ideas were thrown out, and the three continued to brainstorm at their table in the shade.

When Monique left the others talking on Middle Deck, she was wearing her T-shirt. Queen Bee and all! As she made her journey up two deck levels to the Jacuzzi and swimming pools on Caribbean Deck, many passenger eyes were directed toward her chest. As they read the inscription, some had puzzled looks on their face, but most just smiled. Gertie Needles, who was obviously hard of hearing, among other things, kept asking Monique what "trippin'" meant. After about the third time, Monique explained it loud enough for her to hear. Monique didn't stick around to see if Gertie actually *understood* what she had heard.

Sidney finished eating and took a walk on Caribbean Deck to relax after today's anxiety attack. He figured his workout class would take his mind off Monique. He wasn't trying to go there anymore when it came to that woman. He decided if he ran into her, just by chance, that he would of course act surprised, but then he would simply give her a hug and tell her how glad he was to see her again. He was going to be so cool and aloof that she would never suspect that he was caught off guard.

Sidney didn't know it but his opportunity to run into Monique was about to happen sooner than he thought—as he approached the swimming pool area. Monique, stripped down to just her black bathing suit, was looking at him with a surprised and subtle smirky smile of disbelief. When Sidney finally looked up it was too late to turn around and do an about face.

"I don't B-E-L-I-E-V-E it. It can't be you!" Monique said with her arms crossed.

"Hey...how have you been? Isn't your name Monique or Michelle?"

"It's Monique. Good of you to kinda remember my name. What did you say your name was?"

"It's Sidney. Now I know you didn't forget me, baby?" *I know this woman didn't forget my name,* Sidney thought to himself.

"Yeah, that's right. Sidney." *What's this "baby" stuff,* Monique thought. *I'm not anyone's baby. Maybe I might let him read my T-shirt and get hip to a few things about me.*

"So what brings you on this fine western Caribbean cruise? You look wonderful, if I might say so." He was checking her out from head to toe. The black swim suit was curving in all the right places. He wasn't sure if he should ask for a hug or initiate one on his own.

"Thank you for the compliment," Monique said and extended her arms to hug him. He respectfully hugged her back, tightly, but it was definitely a gentlemen's hug.

"So what are you doing on this ship?" Sidney asked.

Monique told him she was traveling with her close girl-friends, one of whom was celebrating her fortieth birthday. He said he'd like to meet them before the cruise ended.

"It's been a long time, Sidney," Monique said, thinking back to the time they spent together in New York.

"I agree. You didn't mention whether you brought your husband."

"No, I didn't."

"So did you?"

"What do you think?"

"I would guess that you're traveling without him. This trip sounds like a girl thang. But I thought I better ask. I wouldn't want to get thrown overboard or anything. You are definitely wearing the heck out of that bathing suit. Were you about to get in?" Solomon was pointing at the water in the bubbling Jacuzzi, hoping she would just get in and submerge her beautiful body in the water. He was having trouble averting his eyes. She looked so good!

"Yes, I was. Care to join me?" *Hold up... girl!* Monique thought. *Don't you dare get desperate. You don't know this man from Adam. He's probably had about ten or more women in and out of his bed since you met him last spring.*

"Thanks for the offer, but no thanks. Maybe on another day?" *Boy, I guess I haven't loss my touch. I'll just leave the invitation open. Who knows? She sounded like she really wanted me to join her. It's been several months. I'm not going to rush into anything with her.*

"Okay," Monique said as she carefully climbed into the water. He couldn't help but watch. He was captivated. She positioned herself and tried to relax as much as possible. She was a little nervous with him standing over her watching her every move.

"Well, perhaps I should leave so you can enjoy this alone," Sidney offered hoping she'd asked him to stay.

"Oh...I'm relaxing. Do you have a minute or two to talk? I don't want to keep you if you have plans."

"No, in fact I do have a few minutes to talk. I have my last class at three-fifteen. (It was now quarter till two.) Should we bring each other up to date on what's been happening in our lives?" Sidney was pleased that she had asked him to stay. He wished he could climb in the pool with her. Instead, he sat on one of the deck chairs. He pulled it up close to the Jacuzzi.

They talked for about twenty minutes, and then Monique got out of the Jacuzzi and they continued their conversation poolside. He finally told her about his job on the ship. She mentioned that her three friends were just talking about how much fun they had in his workout class. He asked her why she never came with them. She said she was on vacation and a workout was not something she wanted to include in *her* itinerary, but she might come with her friends on one occasion and "watch" maybe. He told her he hoped she would. She told him some basic things about her job at NTW. She didn't talk about her family or ask him about his. She still didn't know if he even had a girlfriend. Besides that, she wasn't about to assume that no ring meant there was no wife back at home.

Monique smiled a lot (always maintaining total control) and enjoyed the time spent with him. Sidney shared some light personal stuff with her. It was easy to talk to her. She hadn't changed a bit. When she put the T-shirt on, he laughed comfortably at her for a few seconds. She didn't like being laughed at, but he had such an incredibly gorgeous smile that she felt she could endure the embarrassment. He wanted to see her again. She was hinting about going back to her cabin. *He wasn't ready for her to go yet!*

Monique stood up and offered her hand for him to shake. "It's been my pleasure, Sidney. Perhaps we'll see each other again on the ship." Monique wasn't making any plans too soon. She wasn't going to get hooked on this one.

"Yes, the pleasure was mine as well. I do hope we can get together again. Even if it's for burgers at Sandy Beach.

We spent some quality time together a few months ago, Monique. I haven't forgotten. Have you?" Sidney got real serious all of a sudden.

"No I haven't. But it has been several months. I'm sure you haven't been saving yourself for me?" Monique didn't mean for it to come out quite like that.

"No...but now that you're here and I'm here perhaps we can have some friendly conversation now and then. I know you're married, Monique, and I will respect that," Sidney said earnestly.

"I know you will," she said knowing that she wouldn't have it any other way. He had to know his place. She wasn't trying to get anything started. If friendly conversation was all he wanted, she could handle that. Anything else wouldn't fly.

"So...I won't hold you up any longer. You have good day, and I hope we can get together again. And soon, okay, Monique?" Sidney was genuinely polite and hopeful.

"Sure, Sidney. It was good seeing you again. And let's just see what happens. You have a pretty busy schedule, don't you?"

"Yes, I'm quite busy during the day with my three classes. My nights are free and clear, though." He hoped she didn't misinterpret what he had just said.

"Well...still let's play it by ear. We could probably have a drink one evening. I think I'd like that."

"How 'bout tonight?"

"Umm...I don't think tonight would work. What about tomorrow?" She had to talk to Joy before she did anything with this man! She couldn't believe he'd asked her out for a drink so soon.

"A friendly drink, Monique. That's all it will be, okay? Don't worry."

"Okay, *my friend*, I do plan to hold you to your word. Don't mess up, all right?"

"Giving orders already?" He smiled again. *She was lovin' this!*

"Well...*I have a suggestion*. How 'bout you don't mess up," Monique said jokingly before she walked away. He laughed again. She left him standing there to enjoy the ocean view and contemplate his next move as men usually did. His next move didn't matter, Monique was going to control this thing from start to finish.

nine
The Lion's Den

The three women

could not agree on the wording for Hailey's T-shirt. They did agree to get Hailey a T-shirt dress rather than a T-shirt top. Hailey had worn mostly mini-dresses on the cruise.

"So what are we going to put on this girl's T-shirt," Joy asked the forum of two women.

"Let's see...well it definitely has to be *her*, you know," LaNae said.

"Then it almost has to be *rated* based on what I've seen so far. But I doubt if she could wear what we'd come up with in public," Shellie said.

"You got that right, Shellie. Although, knowing Hailey like I do, she'd wear just about anything anywhere," Joy said. All three were laughing now.

"Now let's get serious. I don't want to spend the rest of the afternoon thinking about this," LaNae said a little anxious to meet up with Solomon again.

"What about this: 'Hailey Corner: Stop In!'" Shellie said.

"Shellie...I think that's a bit much. Don't you, Joy?" LaNae asked.

"No, not when I think about how that girl acts with men sometimes," Joy said.

"Well, I think she would be offended. Not to mention the insinuation of her being a *straight up hooker*." LaNae was a bit more serious than she needed to be.

"LaNae's right, Shellie. That inscription does make a strong statement," Joy said. "But let's think of something along those lines. I do think that Shellie's on the right track."

"Okay, why don't we try to tone it done a little. How about, "Hailey's Den," LaNae said.

"Yeah, that works for me, but it needs something else. It kind of leaves you hanging," Joy said.

"Yes, something is missing, LaNae. It's too short and a bit meaningless as it stands now," Shellie added.

"So what can we say after that? 'Hey! Lions and Tigers and Bears, Come and Get It!'" LaNae winked at Shellie, who just shook her head.

"Good one, LaNae, but it's too long and the lettering alone would cost us a mint," Joy said.

"Isn't it the lion that lives in a den?" Shellie quickly mentioned.

"Yeah, Shellie, that's right. It's called a lion's den." Joy said not totally understanding where Shellie was going with her question.

"So...what about, 'Hailey's Den: Lions Welcome!' It's still kinda rated, but also funny when you think about it. I think it suits her personality," Shellie said with confidence that the others would agree with her.

"I like it. LaNae, what do you think?" Joy asked.

LaNae thought about it and repeated the words in her

head. "Hailey's Den: Lion's Welcome!" She had to admit that it was pretty darn good. Hailey would wear that T-shirt proudly. She was wild and crazy, and the inscription said it all. The wording was kind of cute too. Hailey liked most things that were cute.

"I think you've come up with a doozy, Shellie," LaNae extended her hand to shake Shellie's.

"You like it, LaNae? Really?"

"Yes I do. I think it was very witty of you to come up with that."

"Thanks. I just thought we might have some fun with her."

"Oh...we'll have some fun, and she'll have some fun too," Joy said, thinking how much of a flirt Hailey was already and how much more damage she could do while wearing the T-shirt with that inscription.

"Now all we have to do is see what Monique says, and then I can order it tomorrow."

"Great, I need to go, you guys," LaNae said.

"Where to?" Joy asked out of curiosity more than concern.

"Oh...this ship is pretty big, Joy. I might be anywhere with anyone, girl." LaNae could have kicked herself for saying that.

Joy, looking at her with a puzzled face, said, "I hope not...you've already been in the forest once...remember those lions and tigers and bears?"

"Yeah, Joy, I remember," LaNae said as she stood up to leave Joy and Shellie sitting on deck chairs. She wasn't in the mood to be counseled by Joy. She didn't actually regret falling for Solomon years ago. He made her complete even if he got on her nerves when he acted so needy. He made her happy back then when she was searching for just that. Now everything was different. They were just going to be close friends. She thought a few months back when she invited him to go on the cruise that she might want to give her marriage up for him. Now she realized that he would never give his wife up, and she wasn't going to ask him if he would and get her feelings hurt when he said no. Yes, things were different. LaNae could enjoy this friendship-plus thing she had going on with Solomon and, at the same time, not feel guilty when she laid down with her husband at night. Okay…they were predisposed to do a lot of things that could jeopardize their commitments to their spouses. But frankly, LaNae wasn't going there. She no longer had the need to. Now Solomon's feelings could be just the opposite. But one thing LaNae knew about Solomon was that he loved her enough to respect any decision she made regarding them. He might push a little at first, but if LaNae made it clear that she didn't want to do something, he would go along with what she wanted.

"What was that all about?" Shellie asked, when LaNae left. She thought LaNae had sounded irritated with Joy.

"Nothing, Shellie. We're okay. Sometimes I give advice and it's not appreciated."

"Joy, sometimes good friends give advice when it isn't solicited too."

"I guess I get your point. But I worry about her sometimes. She doesn't always make the right decisions."

"They might be the right decisions for her. She's the only one who can really say."

"Yes, I know, Shellie. I'll apologize to her later. I do feel like I might have gotten into her business *once* again. We've share so much of our lives with each other."

"That's wonderful. You're very fortunate to have such good friends."

"I consider you to be a good friend too, Shellie."

"I hope I am, Joy. I value our friendship a lot."

Monique walked over to join them. She had already changed clothes. She was actually wearing her T-shirt over some white shorts with a pair of low-heeled aqua sandals.

"Hey, you two. Still sitting out here? It's been about three hours, hasn't it? Joy, you haven't changed since your workout? Oh well...suit yourself," Monique said a little more jolly than when they last saw her.

"Are you trying to say I stink, Monique?"

"Well I can't say for sure. I'm downwind of you."

"I get the hint. I'll go and change, okay?"

"Whatever you say, girlfriend," Monique said smiling.

"Oh, Shellie, why don't you tell Monique what we came up with for Hailey's T-shirt since it was your idea."

"Yeah, I will, Joy."

"I know YOU didn't come up with something wild enough for that girl," Monique said challenging Shellie's insight.

"Well...actually I did. What do you think about 'Hailey's Den: Lions Welcome!'"

"OH, girl! That's a good one. Hailey's going to forget she's married when she's wearing that across her chest." Monique was somewhat impressed with Shellie's cleverness.

"Thanks. I'm glad you like it. We were waiting for your input, or should I say approval. We really wanted to go with this one."

"Well, it has my vote of yes!"

"Good, Monique. It's final. I'll order it on my way back to our cabin. Maybe Mr. T will have it ready for us tomorrow morning. That way Hailey can wear it most of the day." Then Joy left Monique sitting with Shellie.

"See you later for dinner?" Shellie yelled out to Joy.

"Definitely!" Joy called back to them.

"Shellie, can I talk with you about something personal?" Monique asked.

"Of course. I owe you, you know. Is something wrong?"

"No...not exactly." Monique proceeded to tell Shellie about her earlier surprise at seeing Sidney months after they had met in New York. Shellie asked if he was the same Sidney that taught the aerobics class. When Monique said yes, all Shellie could say was *"You're kidding, right?"* Monique told her she wasn't. Shellie then asked if the others knew. Monique told her *no way*. She told Shellie she hadn't even told her friends about their initial get together in New York.

"So do you plan to entertain this *Sidney* while you're on board this ship?"

"He asked me to have a drink with him tomorrow."

"And...you told him...?"

"I told him that I would. Should I have declined his offer?"

"Well...what do you want to do?"

"I like talking with him. We have great conversations. But I'm not ready for Joy and LaNae to know about this yet. I really don't think he'll say anything to them either."

"So just have your drink and see where it goes."

"That makes sense, Shellie. I'm not looking to continue anything we started back in New York. He didn't get *anything* back then and he won't get any now, hint-hint."

"I gather he knows you're married."

"Oh yes. I didn't hide my rings. And we never seem to talk about his family or mine. We just seemed to click. He said he would respect me as a married woman and that he just wanted my friendship. I know better than to believe that line entirely. Men always have a hidden agenda, and it's usually about how to get a woman in bed. You know, in their 'den' to do the wild thing."

"Sounds like you're in the driver's seat on this one."

"Definitely, girl. I'm not trying to complicate my life any more than it is. I don't need another man in my life. I'm staying on top of things. I just hope I didn't mislead him in any way by accepting his invitation for a drink."

"I don't think you did. It's just a friendly drink. But Monique...and if I'm getting too personal just tell me...are you attracted to this man?"

"I probably am. He's good looking, girl. We have that New York thing between us too. But he hasn't brought up any of *those* specifics, so I guess there are no strings attached to me at this point."

"Just keep your emotions under control, Monique."

"Believe me...I learned my lesson a few years ago. I will."

"So enjoy his company. If he gets too serious, then explain your situation and what your expectations are of him as a friend. In fact, you might want to do that up front when you have that drink with him."

"That's a good idea, Shellie." Monique was surprised that Shellie was giving her such good advice. It was as if she could personally relate...like she had been down this familiar road. Monique thanked her, and the two sat on deck a little longer before they went inside.

Wednesday morning...

The five women ate a buffet breakfast in the Caribbean Gem dining room. They were going to give Hailey her T-shirt after they ate. The boutique owner had done a spectacular job. The T-shirt was pink with a darker pink trimming around the collar and short sleeves. The lettering was in a velvet-textured matching hot pink color. Mr. T liked the idea of these special T-shirts a lot. He was having fun! He asked Joy if she would give him the wording and leave the shirt color and overall design up to his imagination. This way it could be a surprise to them *and* the recipient at the same time. Joy agreed with him.

"So...do you guys have something for me this morning?" Hailey asked. It was more like she whined.

"What makes you think we have anything for you, Hailey?" Joy replied.

"Because I recognize Mr. T's bag underneath the table. I'm not that dense."

Monique was thinking about the one liner, "Ask me no questions, and I'll tell you no lies."

"Well I guess since we finished eating, we can give it too you now," Joy said.

"You know, I just *luv* gifts, especially when they're for me!" Hailey was acting like a sixteen-year-old at a sweet-sixteen party. It was her special *day,* not her birthday, not Christmas nor had Hailey hit the lottery. This girl was serious about being the center of attention.

"Uh...speech first? Who's giving it this time?" Monique asked.

"I think I'll do the honors. I'm the one who knows her silly, wild self the best," Joy said.

"Just keep it short, Joy. We all want to go ashore soon," Monique reminded Joy with a smile, and she *was* joking for once.

"Hailey...what can anyone *possibly* say about you. You've done it all, if not, then you dreamt about doing it. You're funny, cute, smart, and loving. But once you trap a man in your den, so to speak, you have no intentions of letting him out even if he begs for his mama. So here's a little something to 'ease them on down the road' and into your den." Joy finished and then high fived LaNae, Monique, and Shellie who were laughing so hard they missed the palm of Joy's hand on the first attempt. Hailey was a bit worried now. She didn't know WHAT to expect. That little speech had her mind wandering in fifty directions.

"So here's your T-shirt for your special day...enjoy it, Hailey." Joy handed Hailey the boutique bag and sat down. Hailey opened the bag hesitantly and removed the T-shirt. She read the inscription: "Hailey's Den: Lions Welcome!" A rather big smile came on her face. The other women thought Mr. T had taken extra care in designing this one too. It was beautiful!

"Oh my, God. This is so pretty. Thank you so much. I don't believe this! You definitely got me, girls. You know I'm gonna wear this on shore! I won't attract too much attention, will I?" Hailey said with slightly teary eyes.

"I'm sure you'll get ALL the attention you ever want wearing that T-shirt, Hailey," Joy commented.

Hailey was so overjoyed about her T-shirt that she got up and hugged everyone. It was the third full day of their cruise, and the five women were enjoying themselves immensely. This T-shirt, special day thing was becoming the highlight of the trip each day. Tomorrow was the birthday girl's day and plans about what to do for LaNae were racing around in Joy's head. She knew she was going ashore with the others. Joy wanted to meet up Hailey, Monique, and Shellie sometime that afternoon so they could toss a few ideas around.

Going ashore is half the fun of taking a cruise. Before the *Serenades the Seas* dropped anchor in the Atlantic Ocean, there was brief presentation on the highlights of the ports of call—the Grand Cayman Islands and Playa del Carmen/ Cozumel/Cancun, Mexico—the itineraries, and shore excursions offered. Each passenger received a boarding card that they had to carry at all times, along with a picture identification card to allow them to return to the ship.

A ferry transport boat took the passengers ashore to Grand Cayman—known for its beautiful silvery stretch of Seven Mile Beach, rare and exotic birds, and shops of handmade islander crafts.

Hailey, Joy, and LaNae skipped Sidney's workout to go ashore with Monique and Shellie. Joy reasoned that they would get plenty of exercise from shopping and walking along the beach in Grand Cayman. Monique jumped slightly when she heard Joy mention Sidney's name. Shellie was the only one who saw her jump. And yes, Hailey had her T-shirt on and not much underneath it. Unless you count the white thong panties she wore for *everyone and their mother* to see. That girl was scandalous on board *and* ashore!

Joy did manage to get word to the other three women that they were going to meet at a predetermined spot near the beach around two-thirty. LaNae got sick before then and decided she was going back to the ship. Before she left, and at a moment while the two were alone, Joy apologized to LaNae and LaNae accepted the apology, telling Joy it wasn't really necessary. LaNae was lying. Her best friend had definitely crossed the line.

The remaining four women met at a table that faced the ocean. Couples, honeymooners, families, and singles all walked the beach or sat in the shade. Some mingled in the heat. The temperature was in the mid to high-eighties. A small breeze was blowing. Relaxation was happenin' up here!

"When I first made my travel arrangements, I told my agent that our party of five wanted to host a birthday party for LaNae on Thursday during the cruise. It just so happened that the Captain's Cocktail Party was also going to be on that day. My agent told me I should get in contact with the head-waiter to confirm our plans after we got on board," Joy explained.

"So we're going to celebrate LaNae's birthday with the captain of the ship?" Hailey asked.

"That will be so classy. LaNae deserves that," Shellie added.

"That girl is going to cry like a baby when this all happens. Her mascara is going to run and her eyes will be all black. She'll have you to thank, Joy," Monique said.

"I know...I know. She has no idea we're planning this. It will definitely be a surprise for her," Joy said. "I just have a few more details to work out. We'll be in the Garden of Eden. I'll fill you all in later. The head waiter hasn't told me any of the specifics. He said he'd talk with me the day before our event because he usually had at least two or three parties like this to organize each day."

"Well, keep us posted, Joy," Monique said.

"I will. But let's talk about a T-shirt for this girl. Do we want to say something with the word 'birthday' in it?" Joy said, hoping to get one or two ideas out on the table.

"No, but definitely something with the word 'forty' in it," Monique said. "Something sassy, I think."

"Yeah, she's sharp in my opinion," Hailey added.

"She is, Hailey. She's also silly and fun loving," Joy confirmed.

"Now, she can be a little feisty when she wants to be," Monique added.

"Hmm...forty and she's feisty, huh?" Joy repeated.

"I know! Let's come up with something with those two words in it," Hailey suggested.

Shellie and Monique were thinking hard.

"What about 'She's Forty-N-Feisty!'" Shellie said.

"How about 'I'm Forty-N-Feisty!'" Monique said.

"I like them both but most T-shirts always start with: 'I Am' or the 'He or She Is'" Joy said. "Can we make LaNae's a little different?"

"Well then just put 'Forty and Feisty' on it. Mr. T can maybe do something different with the word 'feisty' to make it stand out," Hailey said.

"That's a great idea, Hailey," Shellie said.

"I also think it reads quite sassy as 'Forty-N-Feisty' using the letter 'N' instead of the word 'and'," Monique said, wanting everyone agree on something. "You *know* I'm ready to wrap this up, Joy."

"I can't wait to see what Mr. T comes up with for this T-shirt," Hailey said.

"Monique's right. Let's break this up. We *are* supposed to be on vacation, right?" Shellie said.

"All right. I'm game. Let's check out the rest of this island." Joy stood up and stretched her legs. They were a little tight. She probably shouldn't have skipped Sidney's workout. They all left the shade of the tree. Hailey walked away by herself. So did Monique. Shellie and Joy decided they'd walk together along the sandy beach.

ten
The Players Rule the Game

"We really haven't
had a chance to talk since we got on this ship," Joy said as she and Shellie stood on the beach watching the waves roll in.

"I know. But I didn't want to burden you with my problems on your vacation."

"You're my friend. I'm here if you need to talk."

"I probably should get your input too. I already talked to Monique about it," Shellie said. She was ready to talk with Joy now. However, she wasn't going to tell Joy about her husband being gay. Some things were just too hard on your heart to hear yourself repeat. She thought she could trust Monique not to tell Joy in spite of the fact that they were the best of friends. She'd find out soon enough.

"You talked to Monique? What did she say?" Joy was quite surprised that Monique would lend a listening ear to anyone's problems when it came to marriage.

"Actually, she was quite helpful. She told me in essence to follow my own heart and listen to what God was telling me to do. If I have my peace of mind, then I'm probably making the right decision. Monique said it may not necessarily be right for Roy. I told her I always felt like all I needed was peace of mind to survive *period*. I guess I just needed a little validation."

"Sounds like Monique had some good advice for you. She does have her own opinion about life, in general. That's one of the things I admire about her. She speaks her mind. That girl has her own agenda, which isn't going to change unless she makes the change herself. I can usually give her input, but I trust her to have the final say. Whatever decision she makes—I will support. No matter where the chips may fall. She knows I'll be there if she needs me. We've been through a lot together."

"How long have you two been friends?" Shellie asked.

"Monique's been my friend for more than ten years. I love her dearly." Sure she loved Monique, but Joy hated to admit that she and Monique had played a lot of games throughout their marriages. Years ago, they were so busy playing with other men's hearts, they managed to forget how easily they could have broken their own husbands' hearts in the long run.

"I can tell you're very close to both Monique and LaNae," Shellie said admiring Joy for her long-term friendships and devotion to the two women.

"We've all been through a lot together. It would take something tragic to break up our friendship. Now don't get me wrong. We get on each other's nerve every now and then. LaNae and Monique have had a few miscommunications. Monique and me, too. But we know what's important in life, and our friendship is important to us."

"I think it's pretty unique to have more than one close friend," Shellie said.

"I cherish my close friendship with LaNae and Monique, with Hailey, and with you, too, Shellie. I would never jeopardize my friendship with any one of you. All of you count in my life. And you will always be *special* to me. I mean that."

"Gosh, Joy. I never knew you felt that way. I consider you my special friend, too. You have always made me feel good about me. And I know I can trust you. I don't have very many close friends. Most of my life revolves around my family, which is okay because they mean everything to me. I know I need to get a life of my own, but I wouldn't know where to start, girlfriend."

"You start right here," Joy said pointing her finger at Shellie. "What do you want to do with your life?"

"Oh...I wish I had an answer to that question."

"Okay, here's a simple exercise, and I don't even want you to discuss it with me. This will be a test of how true you can be to yourself."

"Joy, I'm not so sure I'm ready for this game or whatever you call it." Shellie was a little uneasy. She didn't know what Joy was going ask her to do.

"You know I'm making this up as I go. Just relax. Let's walk a little. You're getting yourself all worked up and just defeating the purpose. Actually, you could have some fun with this if you wanted to."

"Well...you better tell me now before I lose my nerve." Shellie was about to lose more than her nerve. The two women continued their stroll along the beach. Two joggers ran by them. A young child was playing in the sand, and many people were out in the sun that afternoon. It was getting too hot for Joy. The shade was calling her name. Suntan lotion was only going to do so much under these rays.

"Name one daring thing you have never done and then do it either alone or with another person. I just want you to do some thing before this cruise is over. And I don't have to know whether you do it or not. It's something only you can decide to do. I don't care when you do it...or who you do it with."

"Joy...what are you trying to get me to do? Be a voyager or something?"

"That's *voyeur,* girl...and no, I don't want you to be one of those. Unless you want to!"

"No, that's quite all right," Shellie said with a puzzled look on her face.

"Then have some fun, girl! This is just a silly game. You don't have to be bothered with it if you don't want to. I told you it came off the top of my head!"

"No...no...I'm beginning to like your little game. What do I have to lose?"

"Nothing, girl. Are you really going to take me up on this? I hope you don't intend to get wilder than Hailey! Or if you do, I don't wanna hear about it," Joy said while laughing.

"Let me think on it for just a minute." Shellie contemplated for not more than a few seconds and said, "I'm doin' it!" Soon after that a mischievous and secretive smile began to appear on Shellie's face. She obviously knew *exactly* what she wanted to do and perhaps with whom.

Shellie and Joy returned to the ship about two hours later. They stopped in Mr. T's boutique to order LaNae's T-shirt.

LaNae thought her getting sick routine worked like a charm. She didn't want to lie to her friends, but was it really a lie if the objective was *to keep folk out her business?* She would do whatever she had to do and that was that. She was going to see Solomon whenever the opportunity presented itself. And with everyone going ashore, she wasn't about to pass this one up. She would have liked to walk along the beach with him. They could have pulled it off, too, but LaNae figured Joy would have to get the others together on shore to plan her birthday festivities, so there was more of a chance of Solomon being seen. In fact, LaNae decided that she was going to ask Solomon if he wanted to come out of hiding and eat dinner with them at her at birthday celebration. What a surprise that would be! LaNae smiled, thinking, *I would love to see the look on ole Ms. Righteous Joy's face when Solomon walks into the Garden of Eden, tuxedo and all, and sits down right next to me! First, Monique would have to tell Joy to close her mouth. Then Monique would give Joy* **the eye** *that would suggest she mind her own business. I can always count on Monique to gracefully shut Joy up, especially when Joy gets all holier-than-thou on me. That's my girl, Monique!*

LaNae left a message at the Information Desk for Solomon to meet her tonight around midnight on the Upper Deck, their familiar spot. She was going to ask him to meet her at the Captain's Cocktail party tomorrow evening. After all, it was *her* birthday. She was the guest of honor so she could invite whomever she wanted, right?

The rules to the secrets-and-lies game were about to be broken by the key players involved. This was okay because it was their game and their rules from the start.

Everyone returned to the ship, showered, shaved, and relaxed until it was time for their late dinner seating. *Serenades the Seas* had made it to its first port of call, the Island of Grand Cayman, and the passengers shopped in the many boutiques of George Town. Joy caught up with the head waiter between the early and late seating to finalize LaNae's birthday dinner plans. The head waiter had spoken to the captain of the ship; and, in LaNae's honor, he was going to give her a birthday toast. Joy thought she'd surprise LaNae and not tell her about the toast. Her friend deserved nothing but the best on her fortieth B-Day. Joy was going make sure it was all top of the line. The rest of the evening plans for LaNae included a few waiters singing the traditional birthday song as they brought her cake out.

There would be plenty of time to mingle at the Captain's Cocktail Party. In fact, the head waiter mentioned that there were three other people celebrating birthdays on the same day. Two were women who were also turning forty and a man who was turning thirty. That almost put a damper on things. Joy thought they should do their T-shirt thing after they ate. The plans were set and everything was kosher. All Joy had to do was pick up LaNae's T-shirt and figure out what dress she was going to wear. Whichever dress she was not going wear to LaNae's dinner she'd have to wear to the farewell gala on the last day of the cruise. She had only brought two formals with her. So in reality she had to make a decision about what she wanted to wear on Saturday, and that was two days away. Decisions, decisions, decisions.

Monique popped her head in the recreation room on Main Deck. Sidney was busy packing up his gear following his three-fifteen workout. Two ladies and a man straggled behind to ask him some diet and exercise questions. Sidney quickly looked up and acknowledged Monique's presence with his charming smile. At that point he was anxious to get rid of the three. When they saw Monique they quickly got the hint. Monique walked into the room, fanning her face.

"I guess you had them sweatin' to seventies in here! Isn't that what Richard Simmons does?"

"Little Richie Simmons...*pleeze*, okay? How was your day? Did you go ashore?" Sidney asked. It was apparent that he really missed talking with Monique.

"My day was fine...and yes, I went ashore," Monique said flatly.

"So did you stop by to see me flex?" And Sidney bent both his forearms up like a body builder in competition. His arms were buff! Monique wanted to grab onto those "Popeye" bulges and swing on them like they were jungle gym bars. The man was so sexy!

"Was that a vein that popped?" Monique said, laughing. He laughed too with that gorgeous smile Monique appreciated in the utmost way.

"Now why does a sista always gotta DIS a brotha, girlfriend?" Sidney asked, making all of the appropriate gestures with his hands as he resorted to ebonics.

"I'm not your girlfriend...and because I *can*."

"Oh, that's right. You're a woman who stands by her convictions."

"If that means I give you a hard way to go, then yes...I do stand by them," Monique said.

"Why me?"

"Why not?"

"Because I deserve better, Monique."

"Who says?"

"I do."

"Why do *you* say?"

"Cause I *can*?" Sidney said using Monique's words for a change.

"Good response. So what time and where?" Monique said boldly.

"What time and where for what?" Sidney responded.

"Drinks tonight...did you forget?"

"No, I was hoping you'd say we could have dinner."

"Keep your hopes up, Sidney. There's still three days left!"

"You know my hopes are up, Monique. But you're a hard nut to crack."

"So what time and when?" Monique repeated.

"You can decide, sweetie." *Sweetie,* Monique thought. *We're being awfully friendly here, aren't we?*

"Okay...how bout that OZ Club at ten?" Monique suggested with emphasis on the word Oz.

"That's fine with me. What shall I wear?"

"Not what you have on. You're a little scented right now."

"Sorry. I just finished teaching an aerobics class, if you forgot."

"I know. I'm joking. I don't care what you wear as long as you have clean underwear. My mother used to *always* tell me that."

"Who told you *I wear underwear*?"

"Who told you *I had a need to know*? See ya tonight, Sidney. Don't be late? Okay?"

"Still giving orders, huh?" Sidney said, not exactly joking as he began to surmise how controlling Monique really was.

"Sorry, *I have a suggestion*...you don't wanna be late, okey dokey?" And Monique walked away giggling. She liked playing with him. He was serious one minute and silly the next. She smiled, thinking: *This is going to be easy.* Sidney was falling for her like a baby bird from a tree. She'd catch him before he hit the ground though.

Hailey couldn't wait to finish dinner with her friends and head over to the Emerald Palace Lounge to hang out with Zeus for some real fun and games. She hadn't really gotten the chance to talk with him alone for any length of time. She thought he had taken some notice of her, and she had even caught him staring at her once or twice. *Well, Zeus, I'm about to make your day, maybe even your night,* Hailey thought. *No, she wouldn't go that far. She had already been that far and had almost got more than she bargained for.*

Hailey sauntered up to Zeus's bar like she owned the place. As she approached, Zeus looked up and motioned for her to come sit on the empty barstool directly in front of his cash register. The evening crowd hadn't arrived yet so Zeus had time to entertain Hailey as well as to be entertained by her.

"So...Zeus, how are things going?" Hailey was trying to act shy and doing a poor job.

"Not too bad, Hailey. And I might I say you look...uh...lovely this evening." Hailey knew how she looked. She wore a sheer white lace top with a mini-length white swing skirt knowing she would attract his attention. Underneath the top, Hailey wore a short camisole, which only covered her bra. With bare skin showing through the white lace, Zeus's eyes were drawn right where Hailey wanted them.

"We've never had a chance to have a good talk, Zeus."

"What do you want to talk about?" he asked.

"Games. Why do you suppose men and women play them?"

"To protect themselves from getting hurt."

"Hurt? What can get hurt?"

"Your *heart*, honey." And Zeus lightly stroked the side Hailey's cheek with his index finger. Hailey almost fell off the stool again. She wasn't expecting his answer nor the gesture that accompanied it.

"Yeah...I guess you're right. People do fall for each other."

"Yes, they do, especially if that person has a good heart."

"But why do we play these unnecessary games from day one?" Hailey asked. Zeus knew this conversation was going to be about her. He just wondered how much she would fess up to and how much conflict she had going on in her life.

"Everyone's out for themselves, Hailey. If they're going to play the game, they're playing to win. Someone's got to have the upper hand, you know," Zeus said.

"But why do peoply *play,* Zeus? I don't understand why people can't just be themselves. What ever happened to having a decent conversation with a person. No ulterior motives."

"Well...first of all everyone *doesn't play*. Some people do enjoy the company of each other for no other reason except that. And second, people can't be real with you or me as long as they can't be up front with themselves about who they really are. There are no tricks with the mirror. It reflects what it sees. Many of us don't like our reflection so we front to hide our true selves from the world. But you can't hide or fool 'me, myself, and I,' at least not forever."

"So what you're saying is people play games with each other because they don't like themselves or maybe they think other people will not like them?"

"Sorta...but it may not be that they don't like themselves, but that perhaps they are uncomfortable with who they are, or they really don't know who they are. It's a bitter pill for some folk to swallow when they face the reality of who they are as they get older."

"Hmm..." Hailey was trying to understand what Zeus was saying and how it related to her. Did she like herself? Was she trying to hide from people by being so friendly and sociable? She didn't think so. She just figured that she played games and flirted with men to get the attention. But then she had to ask herself why she needed the attention. Was there something missing in her life? In her marriage? Was her husband not holding up his end of the bargain and tending to her needs? Was it even his responsibility? She just wasn't sure. After talking with Zeus, it seemed like he was saying that it wasn't healthy to depend on another person to escape loneliness or fear nor to depend on another for your happiness or peace of mind. People are always looking for handouts and outlets when it comes to these basic needs.

"So when it comes to loving yourself, you have to be the primary provider of all your needs. Is that what you're trying to say, Zeus?"

"Yes...and that makes *you* accountable to *you*," Zeus said putting it plainly.

"I see. Do you think I'm a big flirt, Zeus?" Hailey just had to ask the big question, but she wasn't sure if she was ready for his answer.

"I think the players in your game have to play according to your rules. Other than that, I think you just tease a lot for fun."

"A tease...is that what you think of me?"

"No, Hailey...actually I think you're a nice woman who comes off needy only because she doesn't feel her own personality is interesting enough to hold a man's attention."

"Oh. That's original. No one's ever told me that." Hailey could see some truth in what Zeus had just said.

"It's true Hailey…you have a beautiful personality. You should stop playing so hard."

"I know I should. But whenever I start out being friends with someone, the situation gets emotional and feelings get in the way."

"That's because you haven't learned how to keep things at the friendship level. It can only go where you let it go. So keep your conversation light and stay away from the personal stuff. It should be strictly platonic for you anyway…uh…Mrs."

"Yeah…easier said than done, Zeus. But since I've always kept everything at the friendship-plus level, I guess I could give your way a try, huh?"

"Yes, you should. You're doing a pretty good job now. We've been talking for more than an hour, and there's nothing happening between us, is there?"

"No…I guess not, Zeus. This is a first for me." And Hailey felt real good about it too. She thought that maybe she should be able to meet a man and enjoy his company without being a big flirt. She'd have the rest of the cruise to prove how well she could.

She said goodbye to Zeus and thanked him. She even thought about giving him a quick kiss on the cheek, but decided against it. She was going to keep it friendly but "impersonal" just like he said.

It was far more *personal* between Sidney and Monique. They were sharing and baring everything about their lives. Sidney was falling hard and swiftly. He enjoyed this woman unlike any other. She was sophisticated and independent, yet she had unresolved issues that he felt had to do with her relationship with her father. She was a "control freak," *her words,* and she admitted it very openly. He hated that she was married, although she never seemed to bring her husband's name up. Anyway, Sidney felt like he was well on his way to "knocking da boots" with Monique, employing all of his best cunning moves like a tiger on the hunt for food. They hadn't exactly gone all the way in New York. The quality time was great and she explained to him that she wasn't about one night stands. He didn't press her at the time. Things were different now. This girl was interested in him, and he wasn't about to entertain her with talk alone. In fact, he was more than willing to use his mouth in a number of delightfully sensuous ways if Monique merely gave him the opportunity.

eleven
Auditions for Drama Queen

Midnight on Wednesday…

"I just don't like show-ing up at this cocktail thing, LaNae," Solomon said. He felt very uneasy about the whole idea. Funny, he was so steadfast about coming out days ago? Solomon and LaNae were talk-ing on Upper Deck. Another couple was standing on the opposite side. Both couples had the sea breeze blowing in the background and moonlight in the foreground. It was a night for romance. The other couple, necking in the corner, were obviously getting an early start on the evening. It was a different story for Solomon and LaNae.

"Look, you've done a pretty good job of keeping your-self hidden on this ship. I think it's silly to prolong the inevi-table. Why won't you join us. If you don't want to stay for dinner than that's fine, Solomon. I don't really care what anyone thinks about us now. Joy and Monique don't control me. I do what I want with my life." LaNae had given this some thought, and she was convinced it was the right thing to do. More so now to give Joy a reminder about staying out of her business.

"If you intend to use me to make a point to Joy, I'm even more against the idea. You and Joy can work this control thing out by yourselves. You don't need me, and I really don't want to be caught up in any of it," Solomon said firmly.

"This isn't completely about Joy and me. I want you there because tomorrow will be a special day for me and I want all of the important people in my life to share it with me," LaNae explained.

"Freddy is important...he isn't going to be there." Solomon had never brought LaNae's husband's name up in any of their conversations. This was a first. He wasn't sure why he had. Perhaps it was that feeling he had of being the showpiece for LaNae's dinner affair.

"I didn't deserve that, Solomon. I would never use you as a fill-in for my husband. Why did you have to go there. You know...just forget I asked you to join me, okay?" She was irritated with him, now. He had said the *wrong* thing. She turned away from him and started to go inside.

"Wait, LaNae. I'm sorry. You didn't deserve that. Please stay." He reached for her and grabbed her arm as she began to walk away. She stopped but didn't look at him.

"You hurt me, Solomon, and I would never do anything to intentionally hurt you. I love you, stupid. You are my friend...and my lover." She couldn't believe she was admitting this out loud. But it was true. That is what they were. Maybe they had promised each other that they wouldn't do the horizontal thing again, but he was still quite capable of romancing his butt off, along with her clothing. And she knew if they ever really wanted to, odds were that they would. Solomon was the one. The one she would always love and care about. He was her man even though she was married to another. Heaven forbid either one of them to have a change in marital status. *All bets would be OFF!* LaNae thought.

"I know how you feel about me, LaNae. You don't have to tell me. Please forgive me. I just felt a little weird when you first asked me about dinner. You said you weren't worried about what Joy was going to say. I kinda got the feeling that you were trying to prove something to her, not that you really wanted me to be a part of your celebration."

"In the beginning, I was trying to prove a point to Joy. Now, that I see how it makes you feel, I believe I owe you an apology as well. I'm sorry, Solomon. I want you there because I want the second most important person in my life always at my side."

"Tell me who's first and then I'll give you my final answer."

"You could never be at my side like the person I'm talking about. The one who reigns over everything, you know."

"Oh....that man. Yeah, I can't compete with him. He *is* the man," Solomon said.

"So...what's your answer?" LaNae asked.

"I think you know my answer. I think you know I want to seal it with a kiss, too." Solomon got closer to LaNae. His hands remained at his side. He was close enough to feel her chest rise as she took two nervous deep breaths. He was ready and able. She was hesitant, but willing. As he moved closer to her and his lips were less than an inch in front of hers, he gently kissed her on the forehead and then twice behind her left ear before he whispered: "We'll save our best one on the lips for Joy. Be ready, all right?"

LaNae could only smile and slowly nod okay. She was speechless. He was her man, what could she say? How good it felt to be truly loved by someone. She was content with loving him as well. LaNae was floating so high she thought she could probably touch the top of the world if she wanted. That's pretty high, I'd say.

Thursday early morning...

The second port of call after *Serenades the Seas* dropped anchor was the powder-white sandy beaches, tropical gardens, and clear turquoise waters of Playa del Carmen/Cozumel/Cancun in Mexico. The five women agreed they could get spoiled in Mexico. Here you can scuba dive, snorkel, or fish. Or, visit the ancient stone temples, cities, and ceremonial centers.

The island of Playa del Carmen is the starting point for excursions to the ancient Mayan ruins of Tulum. And Jacques Cousteau came to Cozumel for its "heavenly coral gardens" and "sugar-white beaches" and the "second largest reef in the world." Cozumel also has the best deals for T-shirts, silver, and pottery, especially if you walked inland along the main road. Snorkeling is a must to explore the clear waters and see the jewel-colored tropical fish. The water is warm, and you can see for miles underneath. The sea around Cozumel is different colors depending on where you see it.

Cancun also has over two hundred restaurants, ranging from ocean side bistros for casual dining to elegant theme restaurants. And as far as the night life went...there was everything from rock to reggae to tango to topless among the selection of clubs.

With that in mind, Joy and her company decided they would be among the rather large group of early risers prepared to eat out in the fresh ocean air. The early bird buffet breakfast served on deck at Sandy Beach included eggs, bacon, cereal, croissants, sweet rolls, juice, coffee, and tea. After the five ate, they were ready to go ashore by nine-thirty. Joy ordered LaNae's T-shirt before she went ashore and asked if it could be ready early. Shellie volunteered to pick it up this time.

Everyone, with the exception of Joy, planned to return to the ship by noon. *How else were the four going to work out the specifics regarding Joy's T-shirt for her special day on Friday?* The cocktail hour started at seven that evening. They had plenty of time to enjoy the afternoon on shore and the early part of the evening on or off deck.

Today and tomorrow, Sidney decided to combine his advance and beginners/intermediate class into one large one that would start at two forty-five in the afternoon. He posted notices with the new class time at both dining room entrances and outside on deck around the Sandy Beach buffet line and eating areas. With all of the exciting on-shore excursions, very few passengers were coming to Sidney's morning workouts. He thought if he combined two of his classes he might get a group of twenty or more versus the fewer than ten he had at both of yesterday's classes. He expected even fewer to come out this morning. He hoped this later afternoon class would have a larger attendance.

Noon that same day...

Upon their return to the ship, LaNae, Monique, Hailey, and Shellie were sitting in the Emerald Palace Lounge tossing around ideas for Joy's T-shirt. After they had all done some shopping in Cozumel, everyone agreed to do their own thing. Joy had taken a book along with her when she went off shore with them, saying she was going to sit on the beach and read for awhile.

"I'm kinda happy there are only five of us on this trip. Coming up with the wording for all our T-shirts has been a job and a half," Monique said unexpectedly.

"Yeah, 'think work' is what they call it," Shellie said.

"We do all work at an advertising company, you know. So this is somewhat in our line of business," LaNae said to get them to stop complaining.

"But hey LaNae...we all work in *accounting*, I believe? That's numbers, okay?" Hailey countered.

"Stop complaining. You all know it was a good idea. In fact, it was Joy's idea. So we definitely need to put some profound statement on her shirt. Something dealing with men. She always has something to say about brothas and how men don't always do the right thing," LaNae said. She couldn't help but think about Joy's attitude toward Solomon because he was married.

"I agree, LaNae. Hmm...something about not taking any crap from men. Joy never did let a man, single or married, mess over her," Monique said, knowing she had let one or two men get one on her, but that she was staying miles ahead of Sidney and his game playing with women.

"Boy, you guys know a side of Joy that I know nothing about," Shellie said as she shook her head in disbelief.

"I know that side of her. Joy wouldn't take auditions from any weak man. Weak men have a lot of issues to deal with. For example, if they haven't given themselves enough time to heal from that one *bad* relationship, they can sometimes bring all that unresolved drama to their next relationship. Men with a lot of drama in their lives become what Joy would refer to as 'drama-men'," Hailey said.

"Ooh shoot, you guys! I got it. I got one!" Monique screamed, and she was so excited she stood up. They all looked up half-expecting her to have found some kinda jackpot money or diamond in the cushion of her seat.

"Let's hear it, Monique. C-a-l-m down. People are watching us," LaNae said. It was true. A few passengers had stopped to look in their direction when Monique stood up.

"Okay. Here it is! Here it is. Listen to this! 'No Auditions for Drama-Men'."

"Monique, Girl! You are too tuff. Joy's gonna think we lost our minds. That Is So ORIGINAL!" LaNae screamed. She didn't care who was looking at them now. She and Monique high fived each other at about the same time Shellie and Hailey slapped their hands together palms down.

"That just says it all, Monique. It's Joy...all the way," Hailey agreed.

"I don't know, you guys. It's pretty direct. I hope Joy doesn't have a problem with it," Shellie said knowing she wasn't brave enough to parade around with those words across her chest.

"Oh...Joy can handle it. Trust me. She is bold and usually tells it like it is. She's going to love it. I think it's the bomb!" Monique said with confidence.

"I think Monique's right. We all know Joy can dish out some advice when it comes to men. She won't have to say a thing wearing this T-shirt. I think the brothas will hear her loud and clear!" said LaNae.

"If you guys want to go with these words, I can put the order in today and pick it up tomorrow," Shellie said.

"Great, Shellie. We don't want to keep it with us since we're rooming with her. That'll be good if you could take care of it," Monique said.

"Sure, I'd like to."

"That didn't take long. Now did it, Monique?" LaNae took pleasure in mentioning this.

"No...not really, all I know is that I'm hungry now. We ate pretty early this morning. I'm going to the Caribbean

Gem for a good sit-down lunch. Anyone want to go?" Monique inquired.

"I'll go with you, Monique. Can we stop by Mr. T's boutique first? It's just over there," Shellie said pointing to the T-shirt boutique among the other shops on the Main Deck where they were.

"Sure thing, Shellie, but let's go now because my stomach is growling. Maybe we can beat that lunch crowd who's still off shore shopping," Monique said. The two women left together.

"LaNae, do you want to go on deck with me and get a burger or something? I'm going to the aerobics class at two forty-five. They're combining the classes. Maybe I might see a nice male physique in this new class worth a second look," Hailey said. LaNae was surprised to hear her mention the word *aerobics*. She never seemed to care for the *gazillion* exercises this Sidney guy made them do.

"All right, Hailey. I'll go with you. Joy will probably want to eat and work out with us, too. We'll have to look for her. I think she's coming back to the ship in another hour." LaNae and Hailey headed down one deck to check out the Sandy Beach lunch buffet.

Joy's admirer's spent the greater part of the morning being fitted for his tuxedo for the Captain's Cocktail Party this evening. He rented a white tux jacket, black slacks, and a red cummerbund. It was sized and would be ready for him to pick up later that afternoon. There was one man ahead of him who had just gotten sized for his tux. He heard the owner ask him for a last name. The man said it was Moore.

Joy returned to the ship at one-thirty and met Hailey and LaNae on deck eating lunch. She got a plate of fruit and a burger with all the toppings. She said she would do aerobics with them that afternoon. They had to change clothes first. When they got back to the cabin, Monique said she'd go to the class too.

Sidney's class was packed! There were well over forty people in the room. He explained that because this was a combined class for beginners, intermediates, and advanced people, he would show them a simple power walk, jogging, and boxing routine, including warm-up and cool-down exercises. Everyone should be able to do the routine at a moderate pace. Beginners and intermediates were instucted to keep time by walking in place if they got too tired. Hailey thought this would be a good thing for her and wondered why he never offered this keep-time-option to his advanced class.

Monique sat in a chair against the wall not too far in the back on the left side of the room. She was impressed with the enthusiasm and spirit Sidney stimulated in his class. But these aerobic *gurus* were just a bit too chipper for her. They were not only primed but eager to burn some phat! Hailey, Joy, and LaNae were as lively as the rest of the bunch. Monique didn't have that kind of energy. She only prayed it wasn't going to get too hot and sweaty in the room. Sitting beside her, fanning her face was Janeen McClaine.

"Honey...I can't keep my eyes off that man. I go to his early morning class, ya know," Janeen boasted. She was wearing one of those elastic bands around her forehead and matching workout spandex pants and top. If she bent over too low, her unsupported breasts might easily fall out of that top of hers. They were so round they would probably bounce and score two points each. This woman was not timid when it came her body parts.

"Excuse, me?" Monique said while trying to look preoccupied with what Sidney was saying to his class.

"Yes, girly...I was just commenting on our instructor up front...uh...Sidney Masters. Do you know him?"

"No, ma'am," Monique said quickly.

"Well isn't he handsome? I think he has a thing for older women," Janeen said pushing her hair back as if the headband she was wearing wasn't doing the job.

"You think so?" And Monique knew this conversation was going to get better by the minute. She caught Sidney looking at her. When he saw the older woman sitting beside Monique, he shook his head. He didn't miss a step. This man was really good at his job.

"I wanted him to be my personal trainer, but he said he was under a salaried contract with this cruise line." Janeen continued to talk to Monique like they were the best of friends.

"Oh really. Your very own personal trainer? I've heard about those guys. They can really get you in shape, can't they? And it's all legal, too." Monique was enticing her to speak freely, something Janeen didn't actually need help to do.

"Yes, girl. He'd be a good trainer. I would love for him to stretch my body. I can think of a few positions right now. I know he wanted to take the job, but they played politics with him. He told me couldn't do it."

"Do you think he's the type that would give private lessons?" Monique asked. She could barely keep a serious look on her face in anticipation of Janeen's answer.

"Girl, I tried to get some private lessons, too. He looks at me sometimes like he's attracted to me. He'd probably come to my room if I just asked him. I might do that before this cruise is over yet." Janeen continued to stare at Sidney as he demonstrated some of his warm-up exercises.

"You should ask him girl! He might hook you up with a little something on the side. He looks like the type to me. I wanted to do him too when I first saw him today. But did you say he likes older women?" Monique couldn't wait to be enlightened about this aspect of Sidney's lifestyle.

"Yes, he does in my opinion. He teaches this class for these *older women* in the morning. I just go because the women I travel with are in his class." Monique thought: *This woman would proably lie about her age even when the truth was staring at her in the mirror. Did she expect me to believe that she wasn't the same age as these so called traveling friends of hers? Oh boy. She must think I dated Snow White's dopey elf.*

"And please forgive me...my name is Monique. I'm here with four of my friends. Three of them are in this class." Monique pointed LaNae, Joy, and Hailey out to Janeen. "I didn't catch your name?"

"Oh honey, it's Janeen. Janeen McClaine." And they shook hands about as firmly as Monique expected when she considered how arrogant Janeen appeared to be.

"It's nice to meet you, Janeen."

"You too, Mona."

"It's Monique, Janeen."

"Oh...I'm sorry, MoniKA."

"No...Janeen. It's just MonEEK." And Monique almost started to spell it out to her, but she knew that would be the start of whole new conversation along with at least two misspellings of her name. She opted to change the subject.

"How come you're not out there anyway, Janeen? You're obviously dressed for the occasion," Monique said.

"I did a few exercises this morning with my traveling friends. You know...the ones I mentioned before."

"Yes...I remember...your traveling friends. How old are most of the people in this early morning class?"

"Oh...fifty or sixty. My one friend, Gertie, is in her early eighties."

Monique was dying to ask Ms. Janeen how old *she* was. But she didn't dare. It wasn't that important.

"I see." Monique turned away from Janeen to look at Sidney. He was merging a boxing routine with the jogging the class was already doing. *How long had Monique been talking with this woman? More than fifteen minutes?* It was more than enough. Monique's curiosity about Sidney and this older woman was satisfied. She was just about to get up when Janeen spoke.

"Well I only came to this class to see if I'd like it. I think they do a little too much for my exercise taste," Janeen said as she stood up to leave.

"I'll probably leave in a few minutes, too, Janeen. But don't wait on me. I may end up leaving when my friends finish up," Monique said. The last thing she wanted to do was to walk out with this *drama queen*.

"Honey, you don't have walk me out. I'm a big girl," Janeen assured her.

In many ways, Monique thought.

Janeen sashayed to the front of the class so everyone could see her. Then she just stopped and stood poised beside Sidney giving him a wicked wink and a smile before she waved goodbye to him using her first two fingers. She looked ridiculous. So you know she embarrassed Sidney in front of his entire class. He just nodded at her and never missed a count. The class didn't either. The beat of the music managed to drown out most of their muffled laughs. They knew exactly what that was all about.

Meanwhile...Monique was *bent over* in her chair holding her sides and trying to silence her own laughter. Tears were streaming down her face. This exercise class hadn't been so boring after all.

twelve
The Truth of the Matter Is...

Monique left the other three women on deck with drinks to cool them down after their aerobics workout. They had all shared a good laugh about how funny the older woman looked waving at their instructor. LaNae eventually introduced Sidney to Monique at the end of class and, of course, the two shook hands like they were meeting for the first time. Now Monique wanted to catch up with Sidney alone to see what line he'd have for her about his involvement with Janeen. She was going to tell him that Janeen had told her all his business just to see the look on his face.

Monique literally ran into Sidney as she turned around after looking in the recreation room for him. They immediately laughed. Sidney, upon bumping into Monique, reached out and held her at arm's length. She was so busy cracking up about what happened this afternoon that a second or two passed before she realized she had allowed Sidney to touch her, and in public too. She didn't pull away from him, though. They stopped laughing and were just breathing slowly almost at the same pace. The closeness was familiar to both of them. Passionate memories and feelings came to mind as they re-called that day they spent together in his New York hotel room. They stood there for a moment gazing into each other's eyes. They were considering the obvious. Monique stepped back first and her arms were released from his firm grip. Sidney continued to stare at her with even greater intensity. He was determined for things to work out between them again. *Neither one of them saw LaNae, who was watching the whole scene with a very confused look on her face.*

LaNae was on her way to the information desk to leave Solomon a note regarding his arrival time for the cock-tail party tonight. It was just a little before five o'clock. They had all agreed to return to their cabins to get dressed around six. When she got to the Main Deck, she couldn't believe she saw Monique and Sidney standing together like they were caught up in *Love Jones* or something. Was he holding her or restraining her? She really couldn't tell. LaNae in all of her boldness walked right up to them and tapped Ms. Monique on the shoulder. When Sidney finally came out of his trance and glanced up at LaNae, he had a rather shocked look on his face. Monique turned around slowly and just looked at LaNae like she hadn't done anything wrong. This was going be an interesting confrontation.

"Excuse me, LaNae? Did you want something?" Monique rolled her eyes, but she was actually grinning.

"Well...what's up with YOU TWO, girlfriend?" LaNae asked. Someone was going tell her something and right now.

"I don't think it's any of your business. But since you're my best friend I can let you know *some* of the facts. The truth of the matter is that Sidney and I met a several months ago. I just found out that he was on this ship."

"Oh, you did," LaNae said as she looked Sidney up and down.

"Yes, I did. And stop looking at him that way, girl. I said he was just a friend. " Monique said.

"Is that *all* he is?" And LaNae continued to stare at him. She wanted to make him feel real uncomfortable.

"Uh...you know, Monique, we can continue our conversation later. Maybe we can see each other tonight or tomorrow for drinks again," Sidney said quickly.

"Drinks...again?" LaNae repeated.

"Yeah, LaNae. We had a drink last night, okay? It was just a drink," Monique said.

"Oh well...whatever." LaNae looked away and started picking her nails. It was apparent that she wasn't going to be the first to leave the scene of this crime.

"So...I'll see ya around the ship sometime, Monique. And LaNae maybe I'll see you at tomorrow's workout, okay?"

"Maybe, Sidney. See ya." LaNae said nonchalantly, staring him right in the face with her best "YOU'RE BUSTED" expression.

"All right Sidney. We'll get together again. And don't worry about my friend, LaNae. She was just picking with you, okay? I'll see ya around sometime," Monique said to Sidney. She almost wanted to grab his hand and hold it to reassure him. He just gave her a weak smile back.

Sidney walked away feeling nervous like he had been grounded by Monique's moms. The fact that LaNae had caught him with Monique seemed unimportant now. He turned around once and raised his shoulders, letting Monique know that he was still confused. He couldn't figure what he had done to offend Monique's friend. She was definitely giving him a hard way to go.

"G-I-R-L, how long have you been kicking it with SIDNEY! He is SO FINE! I knew you had a man on this ship! I know Joy doesn't know about him yet." As LaNae spoke, Monique was smiling to herself. Sidney *did* act like he had a thing for her. *And* LaNae seemed to be pretty impressed with the way the man looked.

"No, Joy doesn't know a thing. Sidney and I met in New York when I was at this conference. We hung out for a day. It didn't get *that* intimate…so there isn't too much to tell. And we didn't do it so don't ask! Shoot, girl, you're all up in my business, aren't you? But I did like the way you *stressed* him out!"

"I don't mean to get in your business, Monique,…but…"

"Yeah…sure, LaNae. There's nothing going on be-tween us on this ship. We just got caught up in the moment. We were standing pretty close to each other, I guess. I don't know what happened. I'm okay now. I can't say I'm not at-tracted to the man, but I think I have my personal life under control. Don't worry about me, girl."

"Oh, I know you do, Monique. You just better not be falling for this man. He's too sharp, and you know it. Uh….I trust you told him you were married."

"Y-e-s, LaNae, he knows I'm married. Gosh, girl, stop tripping, will ya?"

"I might be, but you know his type. Everyone in his aerobics class wants to jump his bones, except Joy maybe." They both laughed about that. Monique asked LaNae not to say a word to Joy. She would tell Joy about Sidney herself. *LaNae was thinking they should both tell Joy their little secrets at the same time.* When they got back to the cabin it was after five-thirty. Joy was taking a nap.

"Don't *you* look sharp," LaNae said admiring Joy's knee-length shimmering olive silk dress and matching long jacket. Joy looked beautiful; and her hose, shoes, jewelery, and purse matched perfectly.

"Thank you, LaNae. You know you got it that way too, girl," Joy said. And LaNae did. Her full-length peach-colored crepe dress snaked around her waist and trim hip line and moved gently with her body as she walked. The low V-neckline accentuated all the cleavage LaNae was blessed with, and the high slit straight up the back left nothing to the imagi-nation of what fleshtone stockings wrapped around firm, shapely legs and calves can do for a leg man with wandering eyes. Her ensemble was complete with designer shoes and some strikingly beautiful pieces of jewelry.

"And isn't our girl, Monique, stepping out pretty hot this evening as well?" LaNae said winking at Joy.

"Yes, she is. We would expect nothing less from the Queen Bee of the divas. Where's that T-shirt. We know you wanna wear it. Or maybe you can *let it drag* on the floor behind you when you walk into the Garden of Eden. We'll make sure the wording's on top so everyone can read it, okay?" Joy said. She was definitely on a roll.

"Okay...okay, I know I look good. I don't need you two or a fan club, all right?" Monique said as she tried to adjust the black skinny straps that stretched across her shoul-ders and back in a web-like pattern. Her black taffeta off-the-shoulder mini dress fit all, curved around all, and was bound to leave all staring in awe when she arrived for dinner. She wore a string of black pearls with matching earings. Her black silk hosed legs were long and shapely in her high heeled ankle-strapped shoes.

All three women were ready and impressively dressed for LaNae's birthday cocktail bash. Hailey and Shellie were going to meet them there. Joy didn't know what they were going to wear. She anticipated that Hailey would be dressed in something exotic. On the other hand, would Shellie be too conservatively dressed for the evening? This was a cocktail party on a cruise ship, and not a Christmas office party. She hoped Shellie knew the difference between the two. There was nothing left to do but wait and see.

Meanwhile...Joy's admirer and Solomon were checking themselves from all angles as they stood in front of the mirror in their own cabins clad in tuxedos. Neither one knew they were dressing up for the same occasion. Both men had planned to arrive on the scene around seven-thirty. Only Solomon was an invited guest. The other was coming expecting to dance with Joy. It was unfortunate that neither she nor her friends were awaiting his mysterious arrival.

When the three women reached Middle Deck where the dining room was, Shellie and Hailey were waiting for them. Shellie had on a white silk cocktail dress that draped really low in the back. Hailey wore a drop-waisted dark blue satin dress with thin shoulder straps and a gathered chiffon skirt overlay. Several people were inside the dining room already. The captain of the ship was in his dress attire and talking freely with the passengers as he stood in the doorway. His wife and second in command were standing beside him greeting guests as well.

The festivities were under way in the Garden of Eden. And two key players were about to make the truth of the matter known to everyone!

thirteen
Guests for Cocktails

The dining room

tables were rearranged, making the atmosphere in the Garden of Eden very relaxed for meeting and greeting at the Captain's Cocktail Party. Many guests mingled and mixed as the head maitre d' directed the waiters in preparation for the buffet dinner. Everyone got the opportunity to briefly talk or shake hands with the captain of the ship as they entered the dining room. Several clusters of silver, dark blue, and teal balloons were placed in different corners of the room. Small white lights adorned the greenery and wall fixtures to illuminate and accentuate the room with a delicate dim glow. To the left of the room, as you entered, was a four-piece band consisting of a drums, base guitar, saxophone, and a piano. There was even a small dance floor that would accommodate three or four couples. A few passengers were already on the floor.

Each of the five ladies introduced themselves to the captain. Hailey managed to remain calm and graceful. Monique was thinking if Hailey did something foolish like try to give the man one of her big bear hugs that somehow or some way one of his dangling medals or decorative emblems would stick her in one or both her boobs. Hailey would then scream some obscenity when the pain hit and embarrass herself and anyone who looked like they were with her. Monique laughed to herself because she knew she was prepared to act like she was no longer one of the *Joy-sisterfriends*. But the evening was quite lovely. Champagne cocktail punch flowed from several spouts of the large fountain positioned in the center of room. Passengers could also order a specialty drink from the bar. The captain made a toast to the four who were celebrating birthdays that evening. First, he asked them all to come up to the front of the room. After the toast everyone applauded. LaNae, of course, was dressed in the sharpest outfit—cleavage in the front and a slit up the back. She looked so glamourous at age forty, almost like a queen. And she was about to be crowned with a kiss.

When Joy's admirer and Solomon arrived on the scene, they merely looked each other up and down and smiled. Both knew they had it *going on* in those tuxes! They did look considerably dapper this evening. They both wandered away in different directions to seek out their respective female hosts. When the one searching for Joy finally saw her, he confidently stroded over to where she was standing with her two friends. Joy, along with Shellie and Hailey, were near the dance floor listening to the band. As the handsome familiar face stood before her, she could only stare at him in total disbelief. He, equally overwhelmed by this portrait of beauty standing before him, was radiating proudly with the pleasure of finally seeing his woman.

"Peter?" Joy managed to say as tears welled up in her eyes.

"Yes, babe. It's me," Peter said between slow breaths. He was a little nervous.

"Have you been on this cruise the whole time?"

"Yes, I have."

"I really can't believe you're here," Joy said in a low voice.

"It's really me. I came to ask my wife for a dance tonight. They are playing our song. So will you dance with me?"

"Of course, I will, hon."

"Thank you, babe," Peter said as the two of them walked hand in hand out to the dance floor. Shellie and Hailey just smiled, albeit very puzzled about the whole thing. Peter and Joy danced closely as the band played its rendition of their favorite slow song—"Someone To Watch Over Me."

"Now, how come I never saw you on this ship? When did you fly out?" Joy asked one question right after the other.

"I flew out on a later direct flight to New Orleans. I also rode in the second bus that took passengers to the pier. You pretty much told Mr. T your daily schedule. I explained to him that I was your husband. I was surprised he believed me. But when I told him about the T-shirt thing you were doing for your friends, he knew I was telling the truth. Remember you told me about the idea a week before your cruise?"

"I remember, dear. I never could figure out why Mr. T asked me so many questions. I was in his shop a lot. He's such a nice man. I didn't mind."

"Well I asked him to find out what you were doing every day and then I'd check back with him. Mr. T told me when you were coming to pick up your T-shirts, and then you always told him what your plans were after that."

"Hubby, you are quite the undercover agent. I can't believe you pulled this off so well," Joy said shaking her head.

"It wasn't like you were expecting me to be here. There are a lot of people on this cruise."

"I guess so. Maybe once or twice I thought it might be nice if you were here with me."

"Yes, I know. It was getting harder and harder not to see you."

"Wait till I see Mr. T. I'm going to get him for being as sneaky as you."

"Well, don't be too hard on the man. He really enjoyed doing this for us. He said between making the T-shirts for you and passing information on to me about your whereabouts, he was having some big fun on this cruise."

"I'll bet he was having fun. Looks like the joke's been on me for the past few days. Okay, Peter, why did you decide to come on this cruise in the first place. You didn't think you could trust me?"

"No…not exactly. The doctor's office called the house one morning last week. You had obviously just spoken with the nurse. I guess she thought you were home when you called their office. She was calling back to verify something about your insurance, and then she congratulated me on the new addition to our family. I just put two and two together. I know about your little secret. When we're you going to tell me, Joy?"

"Oh…you know?" Now Joy was a little nervous.

"Yes, I do now. But I wish you could have told me yourself."

"Peter, I wanted to tell you, but I had to adjust to the news first. I thought I could take this cruise and spend some time alone thinking about things. I haven't told LaNae or Monique. No one knows but you and the doctor. Don't you see how this is gonna totally change my life? Our lives? We didn't exactly plan for this, Peter. We're both over forty, you know. I'm still in shock about the whole thing. You have no idea how hard it's been for me to accept this—not knowing what lies ahead for me and you with a new baby on the way," Joy said as she faced Peter while they continued to dance.

"But a baby, Joy? Our babe, hon? How could you *not* tell me?" Peter took a deep breath. He looked away from his wife's face for the first time since they began to dance. He was really hurt by the fact that she had not shared the news with him. Joy could see it in his eyes. She suddenly realized she had handled everything wrong. She could only hope that he wasn't hurt beyond healing.

Joy normally confided in Peter about most things, but this baby was inside *her*, not him. This made all the difference in how she felt and the concerns and fears she had. Still, she should have told her husband, she thought. She had planned to, but after she had some time to come to grips with it herself. The cruise was all the time she was taking. Well, her plan was all fouled up now. Peter found out, and here he was confronting her because she had intentionally kept the news from him. It was a very selfish thing to do, and Joy knew it now.

When Joy first found out about the pregnancy, she wasn't happy or sad. *She was THROUGH!* She could remember telling the nurse emphatically: *I'm afraid not. I think you've made a mistake cause I came in here for a physical exam. I know I'm not pregnant.* But it was true. Her doctor had done a pelvic exam, urinalysis, and blood workup. Her tests revealed that she was indeed no more than two or three weeks pregnant.

"I'm sorry Peter, will you forgive me?" Joy asked sincerely as they continued to slow dance together. The melodic sounds of "Someone to Watch Over Me" filled the dining room. The saxophonist performed his mellow, slow groovin' solo quite well. A pianist started her improvization, and the rest of the band backed her up.

Peter turned his head back to face his wife again. "You hurt me, Joy. I'm really upset with you. I'm glad all things are out in the open, but don't ever do this again. I'm your husband and we shouldn't keep secrets that affect both of our lives from each other. I'm not so sure how forgiving I'll be the next time." They had stopped dancing while he sternly expressed his feelings to her.

"I won't, Peter. I'm so sorry I hurt you. I was only thinking about me. You know our marriage revolves around me. I guess that's about to change, huh?" She smiled hoping he would too. Peter didn't smile. He just looked at his wife with loving eyes of concern.

"You know I can't stay mad at you for long. But we will talk about this some more when we get home. I want to know about the fears you have about the whole thing."

"Okay. You're right. We should talk. I still feel a little uneasy about having this baby."

"I'm yo baby's daddy, aren't I? So let me handle what you can't, okay?" Peter said joking.

"Okay, hon. And does that make me—*yo baby's mama*?" Joy asked, really emphasizing the last three words.

"Yes, dear." Peter replied, understanding the situation from Joy's perspective a little. Still, he didn't like his wife keeping stuff from him. It was deceitful. If this woman was going to be *his* mate in any sense of the word marriage, then he'd better be able to trust her. He took trust very seriously. If he didn't know...then hey...he didn't know. He had nothing to hold against her. But if he found out about something she had intentionally kept from him, then she was going to be in the hottest of waters. Her butt had better have a darn good explanation. Lying to him could be the mistake of her life. She didn't want to go there with him—ever. Cause when Peter Sharpe was through with you, he was through. He wasn't going backwards. He didn't even look back, for that matter.

Peter and Joy hugged and then kissed each other, relieved that they had resolved things for now. The band was concluding its selection, and only one other couple besides them remained on the dance floor. Caught up in their kiss for just a second or two, they soon sensed that eyes were watching them. When they stopped kissing, they walked off the dance floor embarrassed. About five people standing near them applauded, especially Shellie and Hailey, whose broad smiles couldn't be missed in the small crowd.

Monique and LaNae were facing the bar and had just ordered their drinks. As Solomon approached LaNae, his eyes were drawn downward to her legs shimmering through the slit of her gown. He was mesmerized by her profile. He couldn't believe how virginal, yet alluringly attractive, she looked standing beside Monique. Then a sanctimoniousness smile of sincere thanks appeared on his face. This stunningly beautiful women loved *him*. Solomon tapped LaNae on the shoulder; and, when both women turned around, they almost dropped the drinks they were holding. Each was pretty shocked to see Solomon standing there, but for different reasons, of course. LaNae had a *"that's MY man and don't he look good?"* look on her face, while Monique's face bore more of the statement *"I know this brotha ain't cruisin without his wife."*

"So what's up, Solomon? What brings you to Mexico? No...don't answer that. I think I know what's up," Monique said with a slight smirk.

"You do, huh," LaNae sighed.

"Hello Monique," said Solomon, guiltless as he could be.

"Hello," Monique said blandly.

"Uh...LaNae, are you ready?" Solomon asked.

"Right...here, Solomon?" LaNae responded quickly.

"Right here. I want to do it right here and right now."

"Now?" LaNae wasn't quite ready for him to do it *right now*!

"What does he wanna do, LaNae?" Monique inquired of her friend with hands on her hips.

"LaNae knows what I'm talking about, and she's the only one who needs to know, Monique," Solomon said. He bore a devilish grin on his face.

"I guess I'm ready, baby," LaNae said, as she took a deep breath.

"*BABEE*? What's going on here, you two?" Monique was starting to get concerned. LaNae and Solomon better not be getting back together, she thought. No one had divorced anyone's spouse to best of her recollection.

"Stay out of this, Monique," LaNae said while looking deep into Solomon's eyes. He grabbed LaNae's hands and swiftly closed in on her. Monique stepped back stupefied. She didn't know what was about to happen.

"Let's make this good. It may be our last one for a while," Solomon whispered seductively in LaNae's ear. He knew she was more tense than he. And then, right in front of the bar, and in front of a mystified Monique and about six other people standing in the vicinity, Solomon laid a record-breaking, two-minute kiss on LaNae! He started out slowly, still holding LaNae's hands. He gave her four short kisses, one on each cheek, and then one on her top and bottom lip. LaNae just stood there with a real innocent look on her face. Then, they gave each other the marital "dearly beloved, we are gathered here together" kiss and hug. Their arms were around each other in a decent enough manner. Without breaking contact, Solomon's hands moved until he was gently holding the sides of LaNae's face with his palms. Her arms moved, clutching his body around the waist. Then, their awesome behavior got downright *nasty*. Touching LaNae's face, Solomon did a full mouth sucking action on her open and awaiting lips. LaNae responded by accepting him generously. She almost savagely offered her tongue to him in return. They managed to keep most of their saliva inside their mouth, although they were pretty wet on the outside. For those who had the front row view like Monique, for example, there was clearly a whole of lot of tonguing, licking, and slobbering going on between the two. It was truly an *incredible* kiss.

It was time to get a plate from the buffet. Shellie and Hailey, along with Joy and Peter, got in line. After LaNae and Solomon finished...umm...should we say, necking in public, Solomon used his handkerchief to daintily wipe LaNae's mouth dry before wiping his own. LaNae looked at Monique and told her plainly in a low voice, *"not ONE word, please."* They ushered a still considerably stunned Monique over to the buffet line. Monique, out of shock or whatever, obediently walked in the general direction with them. When Joy saw Solomon and LaNae saw Peter, they both just smiled, not wanting to spoil each other's obviously wonderful moods. They knew now wasn't the time or place. They had two more days at sea to get the nitty gritty details on how each of their men ended up on this ship. The seven sat together to eat and Solomon was introduced to the group as LaNae's good friend and associate at NTW. Peter, everyone knew was the *husband*. No one asked any questions. The meal was great! Courtship and friendship were evident that evening. They were having a good time! Later, the waiters brought a small cake with one lit candle to the table and sang happy birthday in Spanish. It was a little different, but the melody was the same. Then the group elected to follow that act with rather loud repeated chants of *"It's...your birthday. It's...your birthday. Hap-py birthday to you!"* LaNae cut the cake into seven pieces.

After everyone ate their last bite or two of cake, Joy suggested they get to the highlight of the evening. Monique wanted to do the honors of presenting LaNae with her T-shirt. Now Monique hadn't fully recovered from watching Solomon and LaNae do their lip-locking thing so her voice was a little shaky.

"LaNae, you're funny, fine, and you have all the finesse of a genuine lady. And you know you look better than most do at forty. So everyone who reads your T-shirt WILL weep. You don't really care. And quite frankly you want them to stay the heck out yo way. So we thought we'd put a little something on your shirt to make that statement loud and clear." Then she handed the Mr. T's boutique bag to LaNae to open.

Solomon was *all up on* LaNae, if you asked Monique for her opinion of how close he was sitting to her. He smiled proudly. This party was for his LaNae, and he really didn't care if anyone knew he was married to another woman. LaNae would always be the one. *She was special.*

LaNae hesitantly opened the bag and read the inscription on the T-shirt: "Forty-N-Feisty." Mr. T had enlarged the word "feisty" and used lettering that came in a bright stripe pattern of neon green, yellow, pink, and orange. The other words were in red lettering. The T-shirt itself was "over the hill" black. You couldn't miss that shirt coming or going. It was jazzy. Just like its recipient.

"You know, I'm wanna wear this now. I absolutely love it!" LaNae screamed.

"You do, LaNae?" Joy asked.

"Of course I do, girl!"

"It didn't take us long to figure out what we wanted to put on your shirt," Shellie said.

"Yours was probably the easiest one to do, LaNae," Hailey added.

"Yeah, girl. I think Joy and I know you. Although maybe not as well as we thought." And she looked directly at Solomon. He didn't care. He wasn't hiding any more. Besides that, he and LaNae were just good friends.

"Don't go there, Monique," LaNae said smiling, but with a touch of *"I'm not trying to hear that"* in her voice.

"I won't right now...LaNae, okay?" Monique said with much higher intonation at the end.

"So...what does everyone plan to do later on tonight?" Joy asked immediately following Monique's comment. She thought a change in topic might calm both women down.

"Why don't we all plan to meet for the midnight buffet. I'm sure you couples will think three's a crowd if we wanted to hang out with you now. Hey, Shellie, want to go to the Emerald Palace and shoot the breeze with our buddy, Zeus again?" Hailey suggested.

"Yes, that sounds like fun, Hailey. Can we stop by the restroom first?" Shellie asked.

"Sure, Shellie. So we'll see you guys later tonight? If any of you has to take a nap, then you might want to take it now, hint, hint," Hailey said to the two couples seated at the table.

She had a shrewd look on her face. She only wished she had thought about sneaking a man on board. It was original and cool. She wouldn't dare want her husband to be here. That would ruin her whole trip. She shrugged that thought away quickly. It was too scary to reflect on even for a moment.

"Yeah, Hailey. Let's all meet for the midnight buffet," Joy said, acknowledging everyone's nod of approval.

"Well, Solomon and I are going to take a *friendly stroll* inside the ship, if it's okay with you guys?" LaNae asked, looking directly at Monique.

"Fine with me, girlfriend," Monique shot back at her.

"Okay...you two need to chill. I know you're teasing. But let's lighten up on what we say to each other, all right?" Joy pleaded.

"We're fine, Joy. I'm just giving LaNae a little payback. She knows where I'm coming from. Don't you LaNae?" Monique said.

"Yeah, girl. I know. I can handle Monique, Joy. You don't need to play judge and jury," LaNae said to Joy.

"Boy, women play some strange games, huh, Peter?" Solomon said.

"Sure do, man. But we better stay out of it. Or at least I have no plans to ask any questions. Let's go outside, babe. I need to take a walk," Peter said to his wife.

"If everyone's leaving...I guess I'll go back to my cabin and freshen up. Maybe I'll take a nap *alone,* like Hailey suggested. And happy birthday, girl!" Monique said finally laughing. She stood up to give LaNae her birthday hug.

"Thank you, Monique. You know I love you in spite of your silly self." They hugged each other tightly for a short while.

"Oh! You guys are going to make me cry," Joy said as she stood and walked over to where the two women stood embracing.

"Joy, you cry about everything. How do you put up with her, Peter?" Monique asked. Peter shrugged his shoulders and shook his head. Joy loved both of her friends dearly.

The two men shook hands as the five women stood up preparing to leave the dining room.

Several hours before Monique returned to her cabin, Sidney slipped an envelope under her doorway. He had decided to write her a letter and tell her exactly how he felt about her. He really believed he was falling for Monique and he wanted to communicate this to her. He only hoped she wouldn't play him weak. He'd be seriously hurt and embarrassed. Strong sistas sometimes take pleasure in beating the sensitive brothas down when they are at their weakest moment. He wanted her to take him seriously. She was playing too many games, and his heart wasn't handling the situation too well. He was serious about having a friendship, or even a relationship with her, if she was interested in having an affair with him. Anyway, all he could do was put his words in a letter to her and hope she would read it with some compassion and objectivity. It was in the Man's hands now. Sidney knew writing this letter was the last thing he could possibly do. It was a done deal.

fourteen
Are You Falling?

When Monique got to the cabin, she found the envelope just inside the doorway. The letter had "From Your Secret Admirer" written on the front. She knew it was from Sidney. She was happy to hear from him, but also afraid to read what he had to say. She ripped the envelope open. She was glad some time had gone by before she had received the note from him. She assumed Sidney had slipped it under the cabin door after they had all gone up for dinner. It was very hard earlier to keep focused and to seem emotionally unaffected by him. Was she about to let herself fall once again for another man who wasn't her husband. When she did this, she managed to fall too hard, too fast, and too soon. Her timing was always off. She had also bared too much when they shared personal things about themselves over drinks the other evening. *But were Sidney's feelings going to be more than she could handle?* She'd have to read his note and find out. She didn't know what her next move was going to be if they were.

Hey There,

I finally understand what you do to me. You affect me, Monique. What we have (and it's still new to me) is the beginning of a friendship that has much potential. It shouldn't be tossed away when this cruise is over. I want to keep you in my life in some capacity. A friend, I guess. I know you're married, but you should know that it isn't as much of a problem for me to be your friend as it could be for you. I really have very strong feelings for you. At this point, I need to know if you have mutual feelings, if any, for me. I can handle most things. But not knowing where I stand with you is killing me. If you don't know it yet, you have my heart.

Sidney

Monique hated to admit how good she felt about this man telling her that she "had his heart." In fact, it was evident that he didn't want to give her up at all. He was willing to try to salvage a friendship with her, if she'd have him.

Until they had talked the evening they had drinks in the OZ Club, she hadn't been aware of the fact that Sidney's feelings for her had not remained on the right side of the friendship line. He hadn't crossed over the line too far, and she'd put him in check if she had to. She left him in the bar when their evening came to an end. He probably wanted her to come to his cabin. She wasn't prepared to go that far with him after so many months since she had last seen him.

Monique was caught off guard once again. She hadn't really known how Sidney felt about her. His note gave everything a different perspective. She never figured he'd be able to articulate his emotions so powerfully.

Their first impression of each other when they met in New York was a good one. They clicked, in her opinion.

Monique wouldn't mind if they tried to maintain some kind of friendship. It could be *good* and long lasting. But she also knew how far friendship arrangements could go. Men don't know how to have a woman as a *friend.* Not being former bed partners makes it an even better friendship arrangement.

Sidney really had balls to write me, and it sounded like he'd be pretty disappointed if he had to toss our friendship away. She re-read the line about him wanting her in his life in some capacity. Monique wanted to stop thinking about the whole thing and to put some control and discipline back into her life again. She was sure the opportunity to contact Sidney might be something she wanted in the future. It had been a few years since her sense of control was threatened by feelings some man had for her.

Monique was just going to have to write him back. Hopefully, they would have a chance to talk about all of this. She wanted him to read what she had to say first before she saw him again.

It only takes a few sweet words to sway my mind. Monique realized a friendship thing could put her on the wrong path as a married woman—so she knew things wouldn't, shouldn't, and couldn't work. But tonight, her curiosity was sparked because he strung five little words together—"friendship that has much potential." Monique was such a suck up for this kind of stuff, especially when it was down on paper for her to read over and over again.

Monique had an agenda that didn't include Sidney in her life. She also had another priority at home that needed her fullest attention. She was out of control years ago and enjoyed every minute of it until she decided to stop fooling herself and break up with the two men she had in her life.

Nevertheless, Monique couldn't believe she'd come this far and was about to go backwards. She realized now that she wanted Sidney in her life as a friend. And so she opened her

luggage to retrieve the yellow stationery and matching enve-
lopes she had brought. She was supposed to write her husband a daily letter about how the cruise was going. *Too late
for that.*

Her letter to Sidney began like this:

Hello Sidney,

*I'm weak when it comes to kind words, and I must
have read your note over about four times. You have expressed your feelings quite well! You probably get enough
practice given all the women who cross your path (smile).
On a more serious side, how did you come to define our
friendship as having so much "potenial" that you don't
want to toss it away. You met me on two separate occa-
sions, including our meeting again on this cruise.*

*When I first met you in New York, I was prepared
for you to be a Mr. "hi and bye" guy. I won't deny that I am
attracted to you. But I can only offer you an opportunity
to be my friend. After the cruise, you'll be a long-distance
friend. It will be easier on my heart. I think that maybe you
might be ready for someone like me. We are very different
individuals, and it will be interesting to see if we are com-
patible in spite of our differences. Hopefully, we can keep
everything at the friendship level. I'd like to be able to
enjoy this without any feelings of guilt.*

Monique

P.S. Just wanted you to know where I stand. You did ask.

Monique wished she had that Ann Landers' article to give to Sidney. She used to read it at least twice a week and reflect on it when it came to women and men and the tendency we all have to take those emotional plunges. Still thinking about that Ann Landers' article, Monique found herself wondering whether down the road she could really begin to care for Sidney. Was he infatuated with her and she attracted to him because they shared some quality time together? Whatever the reason, Monique had no business wanting to keep this man in her life in any capacity. Yet Monique was going to do just that.

The article had made several good points about the difference between love and infatuation. In short, Ms. Landers' article stated that infatuation was a "fleeting desire," whereas love was "friendship caught on fire." If this was the case, then Monique was going to take this friendship thing slow. Sidney's feelings were going a mile a minute. She would definitely have to talk to him about that.

The article went on to state that infatuation makes one say "I can't risk losing him or her," and love allows you to be patient; infatuation has an element of "sexual excitement," but the love that grows out of a mature friendship makes sex so much sweeter. Lastly, the article stated that infatuation leads you to doing things that you regret, but that love is so elevating that it makes you *better* than you were before.

Monique decided to give Sidney her note tomorrow. She could give it to LaNae to take with her when she went to aerobics class. She wrote "Sidney Masters" on the front of the envelope and left it unsealed.

Earlier Thursday evening around seven...

Sidney made plans to eat his dinner at the bar so he could talk with Howard. He needed to talk to someone and Howard already knew something about how he felt about Monique. Sidney thought he had learned his lesson with his ex-wife. Falling for the wrong woman, especially when she hadn't actually fallen for you, was a big mistake.

"I know I'll get over Monique, if she doesn't want me in her life, Howie. It will just be a matter of time. We could probably be good friends, but I guess it's not in the cards for me." As Sidney talked, Howard listened to his friend out of concern for his emotional state.

"You definitely need to get control of yourself, Sid," Howard finally said. "I think Monique might want to be your friend, particularly after you took the initiative to let her know exactly how you feel."

"You think so, Howard?"

"Yeah, I do man."

"You know, I could probably believe Monique actually had some feelings for me if she wasn't so hard on me. Sometimes man, I don't think she even likes me. She's always teasing me and she's never serious when I'm serious."

"Well, she probably never suspected you wanted to get with her. Heck, I had no idea until now."

"You must think I'm pretty desperate to go after this woman, don't you?"

"A man's gotta follow his heart. Some friendships are worth the chase in the long run. You feel compelled to save this one, and I'm impressed. But you haven't forgot that she is married, have you?"

"No, man, I haven't. I'm willing to be her friend, and that's it. I just like the way she makes me feel when I'm in her company and our conversations are great! We are different, but we kinda click in a weird way. It irritates me a little when she comes off like 'she's all that,' but that's not something she does all the time. She is the only woman who has ever made me tingle, man. I know I must sound goofy, but that woman makes me shake sometimes. I think I get to her too. She'll never admit it though."

"Well Sidney, are you willing to wait for her to come around?"

"No, Howard. I'm not going to force anyone to like me. If Monique's not interested, then I'll have to swallow my pride. She's either going to want me or not. Trust me, this woman will tell me exactly where I stand with her. She might even tell me where to go. I can hardly wait to hear from her. I know I'm gonna need a drink after that."

"So if she doesn't want you, then you'll get on with your life and maybe hook up with someone else?"

"You got it buddy. But after all of the things we've talked about for the past day or two, it won't be easy. I really like this woman. Does this mean I'm falling for her?"

"Yeah, man. You fell *real* hard this time. I'm still baffled by it."

"My note to her was my last attempt to salvage *something* with her. I hope it works."

"I hope so too," Howard said.

"I just wished I could stop thinking about her so much." Sidney really wanted to start feeling more at ease.

"Women are unpredictable, Sidney."

"I know...but I'm happy I wrote her."

"And it took some guts for a guy like you to do it, man," Howard assured him.

"Now I'm not so sure I can face her again. I know she'll want to talk to me."

"Why not? You can handle it. Can't you, Sidney?"

"I don't know," Sidney said, his voice dropping a little in volume.

"This can't be love or anything. Not this soon, anyway. You haven't even slept with the woman, right?"

"No we haven't done that." He almost hated to admit that he hadn't gone all the way with Monique. He was happy to be able to openly discuss these things with Howard, who wouldn't judge him based on the previous way he operated with women.

"I don't know where your heart is leading, you, Sidney. I think the best thing you did was to tell her how you feel."

"Howard, this is pretty stupid and embarrassing, if you really think about it. I fell for this woman without knowing what her feelings are. How dumb was that? The facts speak the truth. I have a serious problem when it comes to girl-friend. I'm not sure what I'm going to do if she gives me 'da boot'."

"I'm sure she'll get back to you. I think she likes you, man. Just wait to hear from her. Or are you planning to contact her again?"

"Nooo, Howard. I have no intention of contacting her. She has my note, and the ball is in her court."

"That's right, Sid. She does have to make the next move."

"I just need to get this over with and get on with my life." Sidney was thinking, *What life?* Did his falling for Monique indicate that he couldn't have a life? What if she decided she didn't want him? Could he handle the rejection? This woman was different and being rejected by her would not be good for him.

fifteen
Fessin' Up

The group of seven,

with the addition of Solomon and Peter, were deep sleeping on Friday at eight o'clock or perhaps taking a stretch or a yawn. The late night buffet was delightfully filling. No one was up at the crack of dawn for breakfast this morning. Yesterday's surprise visitors had put everyone on an emotional high. Sleep was one thing they could and did appreciate.

Monique and LaNae were awake but still in bed.

"I think it's time for you to fess up about bringing Solomon along on our supposedly ALL-girl vacation cruise," Monique said to LaNae firmly with emphasis on the words, *ALL girl*. She was teasing her.

"Girl, it's a little too early, don't you think, to be playing someone's mama?" LaNae responded while yawning for the third time since they began talking.

"I don't care how early it is. And when Mrs. Goody Two Shoes gets her butt back in here to get a change of clothes for tonight, I'm gonna want a few answers from her too." Naturally, Joy stayed in Peter's cabin last night.

"Oh Monique, get a life, will ya? There's nothing happening between Solomon and I that you don't already know about, except the fact that we're *just friends*, and not lovers this time," LaNae said.

"Oh...am I supposed to believe you, now? Shoot after the way you got on my case about Sidney! You gotta lot of nerve, honey. I can't believe you didn't own up to your own sneakin' around when you found out I knew Sidney. Girl, talk about a fox in sheep's clothing." Monique sat up in her bunk and pointed her index finger in every direction as she spoke.

"I admit I could have fessed up, but my situation is lot different from yours," LaNae said.

"Don't even try to play me. You and Solomon *planned* this little private cruise party. I hope you didn't think we'd never see him on this ship. Love hasn't made you blind, deaf, *and* dumb? Has it chile?"

"No, Monique. I knew I couldn't hide him from you all forever. But I didn't want anyone in my business. This thing we have is private. I'm not trying to take votes on whether he should remain my friend or not. I really don't care what you or Joy think about the situation."

"Now stop lying, girl! You DO care. You're going to do your own thing, but you do care, LaNae. I don't have a problem with you or Solomon. I'm willing to bet big money that your spouses will, though. Have either of you thought about what would happen if either of them found out about this little seven-day trip you took together?"

"Of course we did. He's the only one who really lied to his wife. Freddy, knows I'm on this cruise. He doesn't have to know, my ex-lover just happens to be on the cruise too. We're not doing anything, anyway. We're just hanging out. We happen to enjoy each other's company. What's wrong with that?"

"Ex-lover, huh. If that's supposed to make it okay, then I can see you've rationalized this one to the max," Monique said sarcastically.

"Well Monique, that's the way it is for us. We're close. Sure, I love the man, but he's not making me do anything outside my marriage." LaNae wished Monique was more supportive of her decision to maintain her friendship with Solomon.

"I see. It seems like you've been doing some serious talking on the matter. I just bet if the mood ever got right and you two happened to get caught up in it, you both might forget this little *friendship clause* you dreamed up and go for it."

"We might and we might not...but he's not in my life for that reason. Neither one of us wants to jeopardize our marriage. I know how far I want to go with this man, LaNae. I'm his friend *not* his lover, and he knows this. I think he also knows if he ever tried to pressure me in that direction, he'd be making a wrong move. He isn't going to do anything to threaten our friendship. Trust me, he wouldn't mess that up for anything in this world."

"So you got ole boy wrapped around your finger, eh, LaNae?"

"No, Monique. We have mutual respect for each other. No one is playing any games. We know exactly how we feel about each other. Everything is on the up and up. I'm not trying to compete with you, girl."

"What do you mean by that?" Monique looked surprised.

"You and I both know how you do men, Monique," LaNae said.

"Girl, you don't know the half of it." Monique showed LaNae the letter Sidney wrote and the one she wrote back to him. She asked LaNae if she'd give it to him when she went to his workout class.

"Sounds like someone is hooked," LaNae said.

"I don't care how hooked he is. We're doing the friendship thing like you and Solomon, okay? I don't need another husband. With my track record, he would get on my nerves, just like Solomon *used* to get on yours."

"I remember those days all to well, Monique. But it's obvious that you are attracted to Sidney. How are you going to keep your emotional feelings in check? And he's single and has nothing but time on his hand? Dare I also mention he wants you bad, girl?"

"I KNOW this, LaNae. I hope when he reads my note, he'll get where I'm coming from. It's all I can do. I'm not having an affair. I really like him, and we do have fun together; but I don't believe women have to sleep with all their male friends."

"Well...I think most men *want* to sleep with their female friends, and they would if the opportunity was there. I think Sidney's waiting for *just that*."

"Well, he'll have to wait for long while. He knows how I feel. I'm not that desperate for a quickie. I'm attracted to Sidney because of his presence. I enjoy him for who he is. Plus...I know I got it going on. I can't help it if the man likes being in my space. I just hope he doesn't get too needy," Monique boasted.

"Yes, Monique you do have a talent for putting men in their place," LaNae said as she smiled fondly at her friend.

LaNae knew how Monique used to treat men. She'd put them in their place without any hesitation. *Could her involvement with Sidney possibly change her attitude about men?*

They talked for more than an hour. Soon Joy came back to the room. She was dressed and ready to eat breakfast with them. Peter wasn't up yet. He was no early riser.

LaNae and Monique stared at Joy with much scrutiny like she stole the *last* cookie from the cookie jar.

"Now if you want me to explain, stop looking at me like that. How come you two aren't up and dressed yet? Shellie and Hailey are going to meet us at the Caribbean Gem for breakfast. Come on and hurry up, LaNae. And Monique, will you get up too?" Joy said not giving either woman a chance to get in a question or comment.

"I guess we'll hear your story at breakfast this morning, huh Joy," Monique asked, finally sitting up completely.

"Yeah, girl. I'm going to tell you guys everything." Joy didn't intend to tell them about the baby yet.

"I can't wait to hear this!" LaNae chimed in.

"Oh...you can't wait. Well, I can't wait to hear *your* story either, LaNae. Sneaking a married man on a cruise ship. That's an original. I can't believe you pulled that one off without me finding out. Oh, there's gonna be a whole lot of 'fessin' up' at breakfast this mornin'!"

The two women quickly showered and put on swim suits underneath their clothes. Joy said she was tired of waiting for their "slow butts" so she was leaving without them. She assumed Shellie and Hailey would be in the dining room early, and they were. Shellie made the last pickup from Mr. T's boutique. She waved the bag in the air as Joy approached them. After all, today was Joy's special day!

LaNae and Monique met up with the others by the time they had gone through the breakfast buffet line. The selection of food was delightful! The buffet had everything! Omelets and Belgian waffles that were prepared to order, scrambled eggs, fruit, bacon, sausage, hot and dry cereal, muffins, rolls, croissants, pancakes, fried potatoes, grits, ham; and milk, juice, coffee, tea, and hot chocolate. The five ladies helped themselves to the food, knowing they would have good, *juicy* conversation while they ate.

"Okay...I believe two individuals seated with us have some explaining to do? Which one of you wants to go first? Huh?" Monique shot Joy and LaNae an accusatory grin as she beamed with the pleasure of putting the two in the spotlight this morning.

"Well...as far I'm concerned...neither one them owes me an explanation. You both seem to be glowing this morning. I'm happy for you," Shellie said as she took a sip of apple juice. She was nibbling on fruit, a bagel, and few thin slices of bacon.

Hailey had a Belgian waffle and fruit on one plate. She didn't like her plate too full. Her second plate had an omelet, bacon, and two pieces of dry toast. "I don't think either one of them should get off the hook that easily, Shellie. Weren't we supposed to leave our husbands at home? If so, then why was Joy dancing with hers last night. *I wanna know something.* And as far as you, LaNae, I just heard a whole lot of commotion over by the bar. Someone said someone was kissing someone. Was that you?" Hailey was anxious to get the first-hand scoop on what happened last night. No one talked about anything at dinner or during the midnight buffet.

"See? I'm not the only one who's interested. I already heard LaNae's story, so Joy, why don't you enlighten us first?" Monique said as she cut a piece of her cheese and red pepper omlet.

"There isn't much to tell, you guys. I was just as surprised as you were when my husband showed up at the Captain's Cocktail Party. I didn't planned this, unlike girlfriend LaNae over there." Joy was desperately trying to divert the attention toward LaNae. She didn't want to answer too many questions, particularly those concerning her and Peter and what they were discussing while they danced. She would tell a lie if she had to. She wasn't ready to talk about her pregnancy with anyone.

Joy had a muffin, eggs, ham, and fried potatoes. Small proportions of each. She was planning to go back up a second time.

"Why doesn't LaNae tell us about her little stow away—Solomon?" Joy was hoping Hailey would follow her lead and direct her questions toward LaNae.

"I already told Monique, who you know was all over my case, Joy," LaNae said. "It's true. Solomon and I did plan this trip. Actually, I invited him. We're friends. And there's nothing else to tell. We aren't sleeping together, and I don't plan to either." LaNae ordered a cheese omelet and had two muffins, fruit, bacon, fried potatoes, and grits on her plate. She had finished drinking most of her hot chocolate.

"So why is he on our cruise?" Hailey asked.

"We both thought it would be a good opportunity for us to spend some quality time together. I really love Solomon. I apologize to you all for inviting him, but I wanted him with me on this trip."

"You did? Why?" It didn't make a bit of sense to Hailey. All the fun she was having on this cruise traveling solo? Her husband would have messed things up for her. I guess when it came to a past lover, things were somewhat different.

"Hailey, I told you that I loved the man. It was a selfish act. He accepted my invitation, *he says,* because he didn't want to tell me *no.* To make a long story short, neither of us wants to leave our spouses. We are having a good time on this cruise. Don't let Monique stretch things out of proportion," LaNae said trying to convince Hailey that she wasn't a homewrecker of his or her house.

"I think I understand," Hailey said. "You two must be very close. It's very obvious to me that if you aren't having an affair with...uh...what was his name? Samuel?"

"No, Hailey, it's Solomon," LaNae corrected her.

"...Yeah, Solomon...that's his name. I'm so sorry. I tried this one drink of Zeus' called the 'emotion potion'. I woke up with a slight hangover. Oh well...what I was trying to say was that I believe you aren't having an affair with Solomon. You've been so honest about how you *feel* about him. You must have *everything* under control. I don't have any problems as long as you are aware of one thing: The fact that a close friendship with any man, who is *not* your husband, can sometimes lead your heart where you don't want it to go." Hailey didn't want to see LaNae get emotionally hurt if things didn't work out or if either of their spouses found out. What she said actually made some sense for once.

"I'm glad you're not judging me, Hailey. I don't feel like I should have to defend my actions," LaNae said, looking at Monique.

"Are you satisfied, Hailey?" Joy asked. Hailey nodded yes. "What about you, Shellie?"

Shellie immediately said, "I'm just a listening party. I already told you I don't need an explanation."

Now Joy was ready to share her story with her four friends, that is, half of it, anyway. She told them how Peter caught the latest flight out to New Orleans. He wanted to surprise her. Joy went on to tell them that Mr. T kept Peter informed about her whereabouts.

"...I politely told him later that his wife had no reason to think that her husband would ever feel the need to spy on her!" Joy was slightly ticked about all of Peter's sneaking around. Joy thought, *what if she had innocently entertained the company of another man? She would have been busted! Caught red-handed, that's what.*

"I can't believe your hubby's been on this ship the whole time, Joy," Monique said in disbelief.

"Believe me, girl. I can't either," Joy responded.

"Speaking of fessing up, uh...Monique. I'll bet they all want to hear about the man from your past who happens to be on this ship too," LaNae said quite content with spilling the beans on Monique. Everybody was going to hear about everybody's business this morning.

"There isn't much to tell. I already told Shellie, and I guess you could say LaNae knows too."

"Knows WHAT?" Both Joy and Hailey said at the same time.

"Sidney. Your workout instructor. Well, I know him," Monique confessed.

"You and our instructor are lovers? You did it with Sidney?" Silly Hailey had already assumed they had a passionate affair.

"No, Hailey. We didn't *do it.* We shared a day and half together several months ago when I attended this conference in New York. It was nice. I guess you could say we clicked. We didn't sleep in the same bed, just in the same room."

Now Monique had neglected to tell LaNae that specific detail. LaNae's eyes widened and she looked right at Monique.

"Didn't I tell you, LaNae? I thought I had. I'm sorry, girl," Monique said.

"Sorry is just what you are, girl, for not telling me. But it's okay," LaNae said.

"Anyway, that's all there is to say. We stumbled into each other on this cruise, and we went out for one drink." Monique wasn't going to mention his note or her brief note back to him. That was too personal. She would tell Joy when they got back home.

"So does he like you a lot?" It became apparent that Hailey would die for a little romance in *her* or anyone's life.

"Yes, he does, Hailey. But he's just going to be my friend. I'm not having an affair with him," Monique said.

"Why not? It's a free country...*just kidding,* Monique," Hailey said, but everyone knew she wasn't.

"You know,...I'm not giving it that much attention," Monique said. Shellie and LaNae knew that was a lie. Even Joy, who didn't know all of the details yet, wasn't buying that line even for a penny. That left Hailey who had bought it hook, line, and sinker.

"I'm happy to hear you say you're going to do the right thing concerning Sidney. He looks like the type who would pursue any woman he really wants, so be careful," Joy said. She was very perceptive when it came to men. *She never missed a beat.*

"Have we all finished owning up to our deeds from last night? This is someone's special day and they haven't gotten their T-shirt yet. Can we change the subject?" Shellie spoke for the third time since they sat down.

"Sure, we can, Shellie. You're right. We can't shirk on Joy's day. It wouldn't be fair to her," LaNae agreed.

"So who's turn is it to give the speech?" Hailey asked.

"I think, it's my turn," LaNae said.

"Then you go right ahead, LaNae," Shellie said.

"Girlfriend, you know we all love you dearly. This T-shirt thing was a great idea and we love you for that too. It has made this trip memorable and fun! On the joyful side, we know you have always been no nonsense when it comes to men. You take no prisoners, Joy. You don't want anyone busting in on your party, especially if you didn't send them an invitation. If they do get an invite from you, girl,...they should know they better leave their issues, baggage, luggage, and drama at the door before they come into your life. So here's a little reminder that you should wear at your next bash...male-bashing bash, that is." And LaNae handed the Mr. T bag to Joy.

"Oh boy...now I regret coming up with this T-shirt idea. I know about paybacks when they come from LaNae and Monique. I hope you guys haven't put something on this shirt that will ruin my reputation. I wish I could say I was ready for this!" Joy said, just to stall on doing the inevitable unveiling.

When Joy read what was on the shirt: "No Auditions for Drama-Men!" she was very overwhelmed. Her eyes were slightly teary. Of course, she had to hug everyone first. Then she spoke.

"Girlfriends...This is too much. It is so me, so succinctly put, in fact, I couldn't convey it any better than this. Thank you, ladies. I'm honored to know that you captured the essence of me and how I feel about this subject, which is so dear to my heart." Joy was totally satisfied. She hated drama. Men and women were always caught up in it. She certainly would wear this shirt today, maybe even during their workout. Uh...maybe not. It would get sweaty. Definitely after the workout, though.

"We're glad you like it, Joy," LaNae and Monique nodded in agreement.

"We love you, too, Joy," Shellie said with tears in her own eyes.

"Wear it proudly, girlfriend," Hailey added. "It's all you!"

After they ate, including second trips to the buffet line by Hailey, Joy, and LaNae, Solomon and Peter finally arrived to eat with them. Peter half smiled after reading Joy's shirt, and Solomon said, "*Brothers will never get a break from sisters like you, Joy.*" LaNae told him that some brothers didn't deserve a break. The conversation got into an intense discussion. Everyone had an opinion, which they managed to express without an argument. All seven were going back ashore around one o'clock that afternoon. Lunch plans were whatever each wanted to do. Sidney's aerobics class was set back an hour to four forty-five. They all had the greater part of the day to spend in the hot sun! When the sun went down, they would find another beach bar or inland bistro to hang out in.

Janeen McClaine was planning when she would make her trip to Sidney's cabin. Her cabin steward told her where it was on North Sea Deck. She'd tipped him well for the information. She was going to visit Sidney later after his Friday afternoon aerobic class. He *did* like older women, at least she had convinced herself of that.

sixteen

Strugglin' to Stay In Love?

"Why are we still in love?" Joy asked Peter, her husband of seventeen years. The two had gone ashore to Cozumel early that afternoon. Peter and Joy were taking a stroll together up the main road. It was hotter than usual and their matching desert beige-colored sun hats shielded their faces from the sun. They were both dressed in shorts and sandals. Joy was wearing the top to her yellow two-piece swim suit.

"We're committed and responsible to each other," he replied.

"Don't you mean *responsive?*" Joy countered.

"I think you have to be mature and responsible to be responsive," Peter said.

"I agree. But it has to be a part of your makeup."

"Yes, and many people don't have it in them," Peter said wiping his neck with a handkerchief.

"Do people really know how big a responsibility it is to stay in love?" Joy asked. She had already started to perspire as well.

"Not when they first get married. Most couples get caught up in the frills and thrills of the marriage ceremony and all its hype. After their lives settle down, they can tune into each other and their habits. The good ones and the bad ones. As they get used to each other, they discover what they like and dislike. If one party brings his or her concerns to the other in the wrong way, then you can have problems from the start of the marriage," Peter theorized in few short minutes. He began to look for a shady area.

"Right, if both parties have true compassion and love for each other, they can change to suit their mate or at least talk maturely and responsibly about the matter," Joy added.

"Marriage is not supposed to be a competitive contest, although I know couples compete for each other's time and decision-making power—about money, for example," Peter said.

"Yeah...they can also disagree about who has to do what in the house. Throw kids in there, too. But Peter, babe, it's not supposed to be about competition. The two are supposed to be a team, aren't they?" Joy asked.

"Yes, but if someone is selfish, they're not thinking about anyone but themselves. They want everything in their marriage to be their way. Dominant or controlling people usually think their way is the *right* way."

"And what about the person who *thinks* he or she can handle a situation and won't accept advice from anyone?" Joy reminded Peter.

"Yeah, we haven't even talked about couples who still live in that 'me, myself, and I' world," Peter said. The two

continued to walk along the road with the many native islanders and tourists. "I think if you marry someone, you two are
one and you have to think and act in that capacity."

"You're not saying couples have to do everything together, are you?" Joy said.

"No, Joy, I'm saying the *mentality* should be to operate as one entity. Nowadays, couples aren't compassionate
enough toward one another to have that mentality. When
there are disagreements, one party may not be as sensitive to
the other. You have to truly care about any relationship you're
in and everything that goes on in it," Peter said.

"All I know is that compassion makes the biggest difference in how a couple deals with disagreements and whether
a relationship survives in the long run. But what about the
relationships that have compassion and love in them and still
don't work out?" Joy asked.

"Some problems can't be fixed. Some people won't
ever change," Peter said with conviction.

"And..." Joy said in anticipation that Peter had more
to say.

"And...I believe a person should give any situation,
especially if it's a bad one, their best shot. If nothing changes
or the change is slow...then...I guess that person has to make
a decision for their own sanity. After all, peace of mind is
what enables us to survive and handle most things in life. When
you have it, I believe you can adapt to your situation. When
it's threatened or you begin to lose it, you lose control over
the direction of your life. It isn't healthy to be stressed about a
hopeless situation. It's a definite disservice to yourself," Peter
stated.

"Then it isn't healthy to be in a *state of denial* about
a relationship. Like when you know your mate isn't treating

you right or your expectations aren't being met. I think counseling can resolve some problems, but only if both parties are willing to commit to working things out," Joy reasoned.

"Sometimes you can't work things out, especially when you've been emotionally scarred or you don't have the energy or willpower, much less the assurance, that your situation can get better. I think it's best to move on with your life," Peter started to say.

"...But you know, there are people in abusive situations or marriages that have drug or alcohol addiction problems. There's no peace of mind there. Why do they stay?" Joy said, interrupting Peter.

"People who stay and function half-way decently might have what I would call unconditional love for their mate. I really can't explain it. It is strong enough to keep couples together through the bad and not so bad times."

"I admire anyone who stays in spite of all that. You got abusers, victims, and enablers all under the same roof. That's got to be hard on a family. It's certainly no way to live," Joy said.

"Yeah, unconditional love is in your bones, in your soul, and much deeper than the love in your heart. Some people leave when they lose it. That happens when the benefits of leaving finally outweigh the benefits of staying. The person who leaves will probably always love the person they're leaving behind. It's hard to stay when you don't have a *loving relationship* any more." Peter said. He took his commitment to love his wife seriously.

"What can threaten a truly loving relationship?" Joy asked of her husband.

"The one thing that comes immediately to my mind is 'trust.' By that I mean the *faith* you have in knowing that your mate will make the right decisions about those male and female distractions out in the world, *if you know what I mean,*...about money, and about the future direction of the relationship. These decisions had better be made in the best interest of your relationship or 'trust' is flying out the window."

"You know when that happens, people stop caring," Joy said.

"Exactly. They start thinking about themselves and their marrige loses its bond...its foundation, and just about everything it ever stood for. Then it can't handle the normal ups and downs that occur," Peter added.

"It only takes one major thing, and with a shaky foundation you almost know someone can just walk away from the relationship with no regrets. Shoot, the number of years invested in the marriage won't make a bit of difference. Everything becomes a moot point—the good times, the memories, the feelings...everything!" Peter said without a smile.

✿ seventeen
Underwater Adventures

Hailey couldn't wait

to dive into the water in her hot pink bikini, the bottoms of which covered her butt just slightly more than one of those thong swim suits. Shellie was also daring enough to experience the waves in her one-piece, white and black, high-cut swim suit. Now she was doing a little suntanning up on the beach. LaNae, in a black swim suit that was very low in the back, splashed around in the water up to her knees, being careful not to get her hair wet. Monique was too vain to get within five inches of the water. She sat with Shellie clad in a black with gold trimmed bikini and a sheer gold mini-length coverup. Monique was protected from the sun somewhat by a very chic-looking full-brimmed sun hat. Peter and Joy met up with everyone after their walk along the beach and quickly stripped down to the swim suits they wore underneath their clothing. They teased LaNae and threatened to wet her hair. She didn't take too kindly to their little game.

Three-thirty Friday afternoon...

Everyone returned to the ship after spending a few hours ashore shopping and enjoying the warm beach waters. The group decided they'd go back ashore later that evening after dinner to do some serious partying in a few of the bars in the hotel zone of Cancun. They asked a few islanders about the hottest spots for music and night life activity.

Monique wanted to talk with Sidney after he read her letter. LaNae, Hailey, and Joy were planning to go to his aerobics class in about an hour. They had to change clothes first. LaNae left for the class early because she wanted to give Sidney Monique's note without Joy and Hailey seeing her. She was also going to mention that they were going ashore later that evening and that Monique wanted to know if he would join them.

About forty passengers had signed up for Sidney's aerobics class. Sidney had made up his mind that he was going to put his concerns about a relationship with Monique behind him, at least for the duration of the workout. When LaNae came in, he passively looked up at her; and when she smiled, he loosened up a little. As she walked toward him, his muscles began to tighten; and by the time she handed him the note from Monique, he accepted it with sweaty palms. LaNae decided to ask Sidney to join them ashore after class. Sidney was noticeably sweating once again—*before* his workout. Well...he was definitely going to exercise—the perfect thing to work off nervous energy. His class was going to pay for his mental relief!

After class, LaNae asked him about hanging out with them that night. He said *yes* before she even finished the question. He was quite anxious.

Sidney headed toward his cabin on North Sea Deck wearing a sweet smile. It quickly went sour when he made a right turn down the corridor to his cabin. To his enormous surprise, waiting for him at his cabin door was Janeen McClaine. She was wearing a gold, one-piece swim suit with a large beach towel tied around her waist. She had on high-heeled gold slip-ons. Her lipstick was bright red. Judging by the smile on her face, she probably has expectations that Sidney had no intentions of fulfilling. He knew as long as he didn't allow her inside his cabin she wouldn't be too much of a problem for him.

"What's up Ms. Janeen?" Sidney asked, as he gallantly walked toward her. He purposely slowed his pace, knowing she was *watching him* and appreciating the view.

"And how are you...Sidney," Janeen asked in her best sexy alto voice. She wanted to appear aloof like she had been invited to his cabin because, in her mind, "they" had business to tend to. Sidney was going to play her like he had the winning hand in a game of bid whist. She was just a bit too pushy; and, besides that, he owed her one for embarrassing him in front of his aerobics class the other day.

"I'm fine, Janeen. Did we have an appointment or something?"

"Well, not exactly," she started to say.

"Then, I'll repeat my question. What's up?" Sidney said with raised brows.

"I just wanted to see you. I couldn't wait any longer for you to give me that personal invite you owe me."

"An invite I owe you, huh. To what, Janeen?"

"I think you know what, Sidney. If you want me to be specific, I can be," Janeen said eyeing him sharply.

"I think you *better* be specific, Janeen." Sidney wanted to know exactly what he could have possibly invited her to do to him inside his cabin room. He just might be tempted to accommodate this woman or be accommodated by her, depending on what she had in mind. He was still a man after all.

"I like you, Sidney. I was prepared to make myself available to you this afternoon. I also think you like older women," Janeen said slowly. She spoke as calmly as a gentle blowing breeze.

"I see. You *think* I like older women," Sidney repeated. He knew she had fathomed that notion in her own mind.

"I know I can please you too. So why don't we go inside, okay?" She stepped back to give him room to open the door. It hadn't dawned on Sidney that he hadn't actually made any attempt to open his cabin door. If this woman by some chance found her way into his cabin, there was no telling what she'd do to him behind closed doors. He wasn't ready for that! What he was able to see that wasn't hidden by the towel wrapped around her waist, told him his eyes weren't ready either.

"Do you mind if we talk out here for a few minutes?"

"Out here, why?" Janeen was about to get indignant with Sidney.

"Yeah. It's little too messy inside my cabin. I'd rather you see it in better shape, later on tonight, maybe?"

"Well...if you say so. You know it wouldn't bother me. In fact, neither one of us would be paying *that* much attention to what the room looks like anyway, if you get my drift."

"Oh." It was all Sidney could say after that bit of information was shared with him.

"Yes, honey. You and I would be pretty distracted with more important things." Janeen winked at Sidney. He almost choked on his own his saliva.

"I understand your intentions, Janeen. But..." Sidney knew he had to think fast. He had to get this woman not only away from his door but off this deck!

"Are you afraid of me, Sidney?" Janeen asked. Sidney wanted to scream out and say to her: *"Heck yeah. And I'm really afraid of what you're obviously hiding underneath that towel, too!"*

"Should I be?" Sidney responded.

"Depends on what you're used to handling."

"You mean you could get kinky if I wanted you to?" Sidney asked, hating himself for asking the question now.

"Do you want me too? I can get into that sort of thing if that's what you want. In fact, why don't we go inside and stop wasting precious time talking about it." Janeen jiggled the door nob to tease Sidney.

"I'll just bet you're a real freak when you wanna be, Janeen," Sidney said thinking, *I am so bored with this tired looking woman and her tired conversation.*

"Well...if you want me to come back tonight, I guess I can," Janeen said.

"Yeah, why don't you."

"Any particular time?"

"Oh...how about around eleven?" Sidney knew he'd be ashore with Monique and the others at that time.

"Okay. I'll see you at eleven. I'm going to take my nap now so I'll be wide awake for you tonight," Janeen said.

"You do that, Janeen." Sidney waited until Janeen had walked to the intersection of the next corridor before he opened the door to his cabin. He heard the click-clack of her shoes even after he could no longer see her.

Ten o'clock Friday evening...

Shellie and Hailey decided they would check out the ship's casino, while the three couples went ashore to sample the night life in Cancun. The three visited a few bars and had more than a few drinks. They ended up spending the greater part of the evening in a small reggae bar. LaNae and Solomon did their his-front-to-her-butt grind dance just because nobody's wife or husband was looking at them and they could get away with it. Peter and Joy just held each other in a tight hug, moving their bodies in synch to the reggae beat. They occasionally kissed—tongue and all. The small dance floor was packed, and frequently arms and butts bumped one another. Monique and Sidney were a little more discreet, although Sidney did have both his hands resting either low on Monique's waist or high on her hipline depending on how you wanted to see things. They also danced reggae style along with many others about five feet from the four-piece reggae band. Bodies were swaying and heads were bobbing up and down to the slow, rhythmic beat.

After a ten-minute dance segment, Sidney asked Monique to take a walk. He had to shout over the band. When she didn't hear him for the second time, he grabbed her hand and mouthed *"want some air?"* to her. Before she could ask him what he said, he began working his way through the tangled crowd of hot bodies still dancing in the sweaty and smoke-filled bar. Monique was trailing close behind him. She continued to hold his hand somewhat securely out in the fresh warm night air. A very slow breeze was evident.

This was the first time Sidney had actually had a chance to talk with Monique one-on-one that evening. LaNae (and of course now Solomon) were the only two who knew about the notes that Sidney and Monique had exchanged. It wasn't hard to act like there was nothing going on between them. However, early that evening, LaNae shot Monique one of those *have you talked to the man yet?* looks and Monique shook her head "no."

The two walked a little farther from the bar's entrance, but within sight of the bar if LaNae or Joy came out to look for them.

"I guess LaNae gave you my note...so...did you get a chance to read it yet?" Monique asked with a surprisingly sensitive tone in her voice.

"Yes, I did, Monique. I was happy to know that you and I feel the same way," Sidney said earnestly.

"I'm not so sure we both actually *feel completely* the same way about each other," Monique said.

"Maybe not completely, but we're attracted to each other, and we are both interested in pursuing some type of friendship. Am I correct so far?" Sidney asked.

"Yes...but..."

"But what? Do you have a problem with having male friends in your life?" Sidney asked her.

"Not exactly. I just know from previous experience that it's hard sometimes to keep certain kinds of friendships or relationships from fully blossoming to their potential. The feelings the two individuals have for each other can just intensify."

"Would this be so bad?" Sidney asked.

"Yes, it could be bad...especially if a person is not in a position to commit to another person because he or she has issues to deal with, hasn't ended the previous relationship, or healed from it. I think you cheat yourself out of the opportunity to experience real love if you suppress your emotional feelings and needs because you don't want to risk getting hurt again. You essentially stunt your emotional growth in my opinion," Monique explained.

"I guess all of this could affect whether you can fall in love with another person, couldn't it?" Sidney asked, not fully comprehending what Monique said.

"It's not so much about whether you can fall in love, but the *extent* to which you can love another freely," Monique corrected him.

"But have you ever crossed the line with a supposedly male friend?" Sidney asked.

"Yes, I have. But I don't intend to get into any serious risk-taking relationship with any of my male friends again. It's easy to get emotionally involved with any man you love as a friend. I know the personal effect I have on men, whether they are my friends or not."

"I bet it's a struggle for you, right?"

"And I continue to struggle with the same issues about men, including my husband. I used to tease men just to see what their response would be."

"Sounds like you used to play a few games in your day," Sidney said, hoping she wasn't playing with his feelings.

"It would start out as a game, then I got more or less addicted to the attention men gave me. Before long I felt like I needed to have men in some capacity in my life."

"Is it that easy for you? What was happening at home?"

"At that time in my life a few years ago, things *weren't* happening at home. And yes, he and I both sought out the extra attention. Then I soon realized I had to stop needing other people to make me happy. It was a definite struggle."

"Who broke up with who?" Sidney asked out of much curiosity.

"I broke everything off. They weren't real relationships anyway. I was just hanging out with some good close friends in the beginning, before we allowed the situation to get out of hand."

"Sounds like you have total control of your feelings now."

"I won't let anyone get that close to me, again. I have a husband and it isn't fair to him. A male friend will be just my friend. I'm not trying to play any more games. I have gotten to the point where I no longer need that in my life."

"You don't trust men in general, do you?" Sidney almost knew what her answer would be.

"I just think people have their own agendas no matter what. If you happen to meet someone who is on the same page as you are, consider yourself lucky. But realize that you will both bring different expectations of what that relationship will entail. And believe me everyone brings their own needs and desires to the relationship table, which are usually based on what was lacking in their previous relationship or situation. It's hard to really heal from each successive relationship when you seek out gratification to your needs rather than evaluate what you could or should have learned from the relationship. People should ask themselves, 'What did my previous relationship with so and so teach me *(or better yet, enlighten me)* about me?' I think a person should reflect on the good, the bad, and the ugly about him or herself."

"You're right. Everyone wants to be needed. But let's get back to men and these agendas you say they have," Sidney said.

"I said both men and women have agendas."

"Yes, you did. My mistake," Sidney apologized.

"Thank you," she replied.

"So tell me what's on most men's agenda?"

"Must I spell that out for you? You are single. I know you haven't forgotten."

"No I haven't. But do tell..." Sidney teased.

"You guys want IT. The cherry prize! Love! Sex! To conquer the unconquered. If women are willing to give it up. Then most of you men will not turn it down. Now will you?"

"Heck no, Monique. Why should we?"

"Why do you all have to have it?"

"We all don't."

"The majority of you do and you know it."

"Well, I would appreciate it if you wouldn't lump us all in the DOG category you're obviously referring to because I'm a free thinker and I act independently," Sidney said. He was going to defend himself.

"So you put on acts?"

"There you go twisting my words around again."

"No, I didn't. You said you put on an act."

"I said I *act independently* of others. It's a little different," Sidney said.

"I was just being me again. Aren't you used to it yet?" Monique asked.

"I'm not so sure I can get used to that *kidding* side of you."

"Sure you can, Sidney. You seem like the tolerant type to me."

"So what's the main thing on most women's agenda?" Sidney asked Monique. He felt like she would probably have the lowdown on this too.

"Women are funny...some of us just want to be loved and are more than willing to invest our time and love in the man of our choice. Other women simply want a man to spend his time and money on them because they think as women they got it that way."

"I've met quite a few of the second type in my life. Always looking for a handout," Sidney said.

"Well, I know a few good women who are like the first type and their men haven't a 'K'-clue about what it means to be loved by a woman who really knows how to love in a mature and responsible manner. My friends all ended up getting emotionally scarred messing around with men who don't know how to appreciate a woman's love for them."

"There are no guarantees when it comes to relationships, Monique," Sidney said.

"Don't I know," Monique added.

"Can we discuss something else now. Like what you wrote in this note?" Sidney pulled the folded piece of paper from his pants' pocket and held it with two fingers. Monique was obviously trying to avoid having a serious talk about their possible friendship.

"What's to discuss? I know you are attracted to me and that I affect you. I'm not completely sure what that means, though." Monique rambled on to reduce the uneasy feelings that were creeping up on her as they changed the subject. She went on to say, "...And you want me as your friend in some capacity...and oh...I forgot, I have your heart."

"Are you making fun of me and my feelings for you? Because if you are, I won't waste your time. I'm nobody's fool, Monique." Now Sidney was irritated. He didn't appreciate her quick summarization of their situation. He was very serious about what he wrote, and she owed him a little respect for his sincerity in expressing his feelings.

"No...I wasn't making fun of you, Sidney. I'm flattered that you feel the way you do. I told you I was attracted to you as well. But remember, I will protect my heart at all cost. I would love to have a friendship with you, but I won't give you any fringe benefits and I don't expect any from you. Friends will be friends and lovers will be lovers. Don't be mixing the two up, okay?"

"There you go with that controlling tongue of yours, again," Sidney said sarcastically.

"You can say anything you want, but consider yourself forewarned and please don't take me the wrong way. I don't play games when it comes to the feelings men and women have for each other. I've been there and done that, Sidney. It's easy to have an affair. Playing with someone's heart is not a game. The heart is too sacred for that."

"Sacred...huh?" Sidney was confused.

"Yes, sacred. Now, truth or dare?" Monique asked Sidney. She changed the subject so fast that Sidney didn't bother to ask her for an explanation. He merely answered her question.

"Dare...but what game are we playing now?"

"Okay...I dare you to take off the underwear I'm not supposed to know if you're wearing. Fold them up neatly and then throw them out into the water." They were walking along the beach in the vicinity of the bar but now they were closer to the water. It splashed up a few inches from where they were standing.

"Are you daring me?" Sidney asked.

"Yes I am," Monique said.

"If I take you up on your dare, you have to tell me the truth when I ask you my question." *Oh boy*, Monique thought. She hadn't expected Sidney to challenge her. She was in the habit of teasing him but she didn't handle teasing too well when the joke was about to be on her.

"Okay Sidney, what's your question?" Monique asked determined to be as brave as she could be.

"Oh...not so fast, missy. I'm going to take you up on your dare first." Sidney proceeded to kick off his sandals, undo his belt, and unzip his pants. He pulled his pants down. Then took off his underwear. Luckily, his outer shirt was long enough to cover up the family jewels. As Monique watched every move Sidney made, she was pleasantly surprised by how neatly he folded up the black silk boxers he was wearing. He stood in front of her grinning. Monique's stomach quivered. Was she slightly aroused by the fact that she was within reach of this man's nude firm buttocks? Sidney quickly threw his boxer shorts into the ocean, he walked the few steps back to Monique.

"My turn now. Are you ready for my question?" Sidney purposely said in a low voice.

"Not really...but let's get it over with," Monique replied.

"Okay. Then here's my question: Do you want me to kiss you tonight? You have to give me an honest answer, remember? And if you say yes, you know what my next move is going to be?" Sidney said without taking his smiling eyes off Monique.

"Oh...really? Well yes. I do want you to kiss me," Monique said. She couldn't believe she was being this honest. *Of course she wanted the man to kiss her!* She'd be a fool not to. He had already proven how good he was with his lips back in New York. And although she knew she wasn't supposed to be going back for seconds, she certainly couldn't pass up the opportunity. She began to regret that she started this truth or dare game for sure now.

"Then just stand there and don't move. You don't have to do a thing, Monique," Sidney whispered as he slowly closed the gap between them. Now...Sidney knew he hadn't put his slacks, shoes, or sandals back on. However, Monique had forgotten about that when she gave her consent to be kissed. Therefore, she was totally unprepared for what happened next! First soft lips touched her lips, followed by thick firm hips pressing up against her body. Now you know Monique couldn't help but feel his member up against her body. Then just to make sure she did, Sidney moved it, and shifted it, *and repositioned* it appropriately up, down, and around Monique's mid-section. He did it slowly and meticulously as they sensuously kissed for a few moments. Sidney's stunt was so powerful and intense that Monique let her body totally relax to a point that she fell almost faint-like into his arms. Sidney steadied himself as most of Monique's body weight shifted onto him when they finished the kiss with a hug. *"Yes!"* Monique thought she had heard Sidney murmur to himself. Monique didn't care. She was much too lightheaded to ask him what the heck he was *"yessing"* about.

They found a secluded area. Monique was disappointed at allowing herself to *go there*...and with Sidney of all people. She was convinced that she wouldn't. She even thought about what Joy would say: *Don't go there unless you're going to go there.* Monique wasn't going to tell her sisterfriends about this until *she* was ready.

About three in the morning on Saturday...

Shellie had finally decided what daring feat she was both willing and apprehensive about carrying out. It was so never-thought-of-by-her that she couldn't believe she had listened to Joy about doing something this crazy in the first place. She had to tell someone. Who else could she tell but the famous-for-fun-n-games, *Hailey Woods.*

Hailey was interested and ready to do it! She thought the whole idea was great. What Hailey didn't tell Shellie was that she had also asked Zeus to join them just to liven things up a bit. After all, Shellie liked talking to Zeus so Hailey figured there probably wouldn't be a problem.

It was set for three-thirty Saturday in the wee hours in the morning. Shellie was going to meet Hailey at the Jacuzzi pool. Few people would be outside on deck at that time of night so they would have the whole pool to themselves.

Shellie didn't tell Hailey she intended to skinny dip in the Jacuzzi because she was slightly embarrassed for having the desire to do such a thing. She knew Hailey could help her make up her mind and build up the nerve she needed to pull this off. Hailey was eager and excited.

When the three showed up at the Jacuzzi pool wearing their swim suits, slippers, and terry-cloth robes, they all laughed. Shellie was mad at Hailey a little for inviting Zeus, but she quickly got over that. Zeus got someone to handle the last hour of clean-up in order to meet with the two women. He brought along two bottles of red wine, three wine goblets, and a portable CD player.

They were going through with it. It was all or none. The jets of the water shooting out from different directions from all sides of the lighted pool continued to bubble. The temperature of the water was hot—about a hundred and two degrees. They wouldn't be in there very long. Maximum fifteen to twenty minutes.

Shellie got into the Jacuzzi first and then removed her swim suit. The bubbling water covered her body. She tossed the wet one-piece suit at Zeus, striking him lightly in the face.

Hailey couldn't believe this "A#1 Wife" was so free-spirited with her body. Planning to enjoy the experience herself, she climbed in next and did the same. Zeus was in heaven. This was a first for him. Two women nude in a Jacuzzi? It was every man's dream come true. The Wizard of Oz sent Zeus home to Kansas and he didn't travel alone.

Zeus was last and, being the clown that he truly was, he stepped out of his swimming trunks and stood there for a second or two with his manhood glistening in the moonlight. It happened so fast that the two women looked at each other first, screamed, and then took a second look at Zeus with their mouths wide open.

They rotated positions in the pool to take full advantage of the jet streams that hit their bodies in different spots. Zeus' music was slow and easy. Shellie enjoyed the feel of the water shooting between her legs. She laid back, looking up at the moonlit sky and allowing the tranquility and warmth of the water to soothe her mind and body. Shellie had managed to pull off her underwater adventure without any complications. She couldn't wait to tell Joy and the others what they had missed out on.

The wine did an adequate job of relaxing everyone, especially Hailey and Zeus, who were looking at each other quite attentively as the water bubbled around them. When Zeus volunteered to walk both women back to their cabins, Shellie declined his offer. Hailey didn't. When she and Zeus arrived at her cabin, Hailey decided to give Zeus a quick kiss on the cheek. Being that close to each other and relaxed as much as they both were made it more of a challenge to keep it strictly on the friendly side, if you know what I mean. Needless to say, Zeus never made it back to his cabin until just before daylight began to show.

eighteen
Last Night at Sea

Just before daybreak Saturday morning...

Just about every-one slept in on Saturday, except Solomon and LaNae, who got up to meet each other on deck to watch the sun rise. LaNae managed to get out of the cabin without disturbing a lightly snoring Monique. The three couples didn't return to the ship until just before *Serenades the Seas* sounded its departure horn to indicate it was heading back to New Orleans. Sidney and Monique were the last to get on board. The other two couples didn't bother to look for them when they finally noticed the two had left the reggae bar earlier. LaNae, with Peter's input, was able to convince an overly concerned Joy that if Monique and Sidney were foolish enough to miss the last ferry boat back to the ship, they must have alternative options to get themselves back home. LaNae wasn't babysitting any adults, especially when she thought about where they were and what they were probably doing that made them lose track of time and their whereabouts. Joy, however, didn't relax until the two walked up to her. They had re-boarded the ship earlier. Sidney had his arms comfortably resting across Monique's neck and shoulders as the two stood before Joy. LaNae looked at Joy as if to say *I told you so.* Peter tried to hug his wife to relax her, but Joy was so mad at Sidney and Monique for making her worry that she pulled away from him. Peter gave Joy a subtle *you better stop tripping right now look,* and she knew her next move had better be to straighten up her face and get rid of the attitude. Peter wasn't playing any games with Joy over such an inconsequential incident. Joy knew she was on borrowed time with all that she had kept from him, so a few minutes later, she chilled out.

Janeen McClaine was so pissed at Sidney for standing her up that she was ready to put a hurtin' on somebody. She knocked and then waited at his cabin door a good fifteen minutes before leaving at precisely eleven-fifteen Friday evening. She was so mad she took her bright red lipstick and wrote "Sidney Masters is a Jerk and a DOG!!!" on his cabin door for everyone to see. She wasn't going to be the last woman to be played by him. She was through trying to impress younger men who could never appreciate what she had to offer as an older, *experienced* woman. She had no plans to attend his workout class the next day either. He did her wrong and all she did was try to give him a little something and get a little something back for her time and effort. What nerve he had to play her that way!

LaNae and Solomon watched the sun come up in the horizon as they stood on the Upper Deck along with about three other couples. It wasn't too romantic because they both knew all good things were about to come to an end. They chatted lightly about the week's events and even laughed about pulling it all off.

"I don't know why I don't feel guilty about spending this time with you, Solomon," LaNae said.

"You shouldn't. We're friends, and we know we have responsibilities at home. I'm not real happy about lying to my wife, but she could never understand what you mean to me and how it doesn't threaten the feelings I have for her OR our marriage," Solomon said.

"Well, I wouldn't say you're not totally unaffected by having me in your life, Solomon," LaNae said to be honest with him.

"I guess you're right, but I don't want to divorce my wife; and I know you won't get a divorce either, so here we are. I can love you and still feel right about it."

"That you can do, Solomon. What you can't do is tend to me when we get back to NTW. You'll just tell on yourself. Pretty soon you won't be able to hide the fact that I'm an important person in your life."

"I guess you have a point. As long as I know we'll remain friends, I'm content. I'm not trying to have an affair. We've both been down that painful road before. Besides...I almost lost your friendship when we broke up."

"I know. I don't want that kind of relationship with you either. I consider you a friend, and I expect you keep everything you do at the friendship level. It's what I plan to do. I love my husband. I guess I love you in a different way. I would like to know that my feelings are under control enough that I can look at Freddy without him reading through me. He can always tell when I have someone else on my mind. I think he knows about you, but he won't discuss it with me. I don't need any more stress in my life," LaNae said firmly.

"I feel confident that we can be friends. This trip was a good one. I have no regrets about what I did with you, especially that fantastic kiss I laid on you. You really liked it, didn't you?" Solomon boasted.

"Yes, I did. It was your last kiss, you know. I don't plan to get that intimate with you again. I'm going to try to walk a straight line. If I feel like you aren't, then I'll be out of your life for the last and final time. Do you understand me?" LaNae was serious. As Solomon watched her stare at the ocean, he could tell there was something different about her and the way she spoke without looking him directly in the face.

"Yes, I do, LaNae. I wouldn't do anything to jeopardize our friendship ever again," Solomon stated. His response was quick and to the point.

"Thank you for saying that. I appreciate your honesty. I know I can trust you not to exploit the feelings I have for you," LaNae said.

"Let's get something to eat," Solomon suggested. It was almost close to seven in the morning. The two headed for the dining room for an early breakfast.

When Sidney got to his cabin door around two-thirty in the morning, he couldn't believe what was written on the door. He knew everyone had read it and his coworkers would tease him about it for days. He quickly grabbed a towel from the bathroom, soaked it with alcohol, and attempted to wipe the wording off the door. After a few minutes, the door was somewhat clean, but smudges of the words "Sidney" and "DOG" remained faintly. If he saw Janeen McClaine on this ship one more time, he was going to tell her how tired she really had to be to think he'd ever give her the time of day. He was happy Monique hadn't seen the writing on his door. Her mind would run wild and then she, too, would tease him for awhile. He could see it now. Monique would probably purchase several shades of red lipstick and mail one shade to him for the next six weeks as a reminder of how being a player could never pay off.

Solomon and LaNae met up with Joy and Peter at the entrance to the Caribbean Gem. Hailey and Shellie were already seated at the table. They had just come back from the buffet line. The other four followed suit and they soon returned with their plates full. No one inquired about whether Monique would be joining them.

"So do you want to tell her or should I," Hailey said, looking at Shellie then turning to look at Joy.

"We are in mixed company. Perhaps we should wait until later," Shellie responded.

"Wait to tell me what? I hope you didn't let Hailey talk you into doing anything too wild last night when we went ashore," Joy said to Shellie.

"Oh, I think it was the other way around," Hailey said.

"What are you talking about Hailey?" Joy asked.

"I think I'll let Shellie tell you. After all it was her idea. I only asked Zeus to join us. We had a real good time this morning too," Hailey briefly stated. Joy was intrigued, and she couldn't help wondering what the three of them did last night.

"Alright, spill it Shellie. Let's hear it, you guys. I can't wait to hear this!" LaNae said with anticipation. If that bartender Zeus had any part to play in it, she knew it had to be pretty wild. And Hailey obviously couldn't wait to tell them what happened.

"Well..." Shellie began, "It all started when Joy and I were taking a walk on the beach on Thursday. She said I should do something that I had never done before in my life. And I did it last night..."

"You mean you did it this morning, Shellie," Hailey said with devious grin on her face.

"Oh shoot, Shellie, what did you and Hailey...and I still can't believe you got Zeus in on it...what did you all do? Tell us!" an impatient LaNae said.

"I'm not so sure I'm ready for this. I hope it's not R-rated," Joy commented.

"It has to be rated, Joy, if Hailey was involved. You can almost be assured it won't be G." Then she added, "Just pickin' with you, Hailey."

"Hey, I'm an innocent bystander for once in my life. This wasn't my idea...I was asked to participate. You can bet if it were my idea, I would have invited about three more men and we'd have moved the party to my cabin afterwards."

"Sound like an orgy to me, man," Solomon said to Peter who agreed by nodding.

"An orgy! Shellie, have you lost your mind! You didn't let Hailey give you any bright ideas on what to do, did you? This was supposed to be your idea, not hers," Joy said, her voice slightly raised. She almost didn't want to know what the three of them had done.

"Relax, Joy. It wasn't an orgy. It was only me, Hailey, and Zeus. The idea was all mine and I only asked Hailey to join me cause I thought I might change my mind. *She* decided to invite Zeus, and I'm glad she did. We had a good conversation and a lot of fun. Zeus kept us laughing the whole night...I mean morning."

"Morning? Like *this* morning?" Joy asked.

"Yes, girlfriend. We got started around three-ish. We wanted to have the Jacuzzi all to ourselves." Hailey took the lead and began to explain.

"Jacuzzi? Oh, I know this has got to be good." LaNae had stopped eating and leaned across the table toward Shellie.

"Yeah, I had never been in a Jacuzzi nude, and decided I wanted to try it. It was supposed to be just Hailey and me, hint, hint." Shellie lightly pushed Hailey twice with her index finger on the back of her shoulders. "But I should have known how far Ms. Excitement might go. When Zeus showed up I almost panicked and really changed my mind. I'm glad I didn't."

"You mean to tell me that you were in the Jacuzzi on this ship *butt naked* with Hailey and Zeus? I don't believe it!" Joy said admiring her friend for coming up with the idea.

"Yes she was, Joy. She got in first and just took off her swim suit like it was nothing. Even I was shocked! And Shellie...when you threw the darn thing and it hit Zeus in the face, I almost died laughing," Hailey said. "Now tell everyone the highlight of the evening, Shellie."

"Well...the highlight of my evening...I mean...Hailey's and my evening...was when Zeus let his trunks drop right in front of our eyes and just stood there naked for us a to get a full look at his you know what, girl!" Shellie said in an elevated voice.

"You're lying, Shellie!" Both LaNae and Joy screamed. The two men just shook their heads. They were quite jealous. They had to hand it to this Zeus guy who got a chance to do the Jacuzzi thing with not one, but two beautiful women, and they were naked too? They gave him much credit for wanting to seize the opportunity to get buck wild to the max.

Hailey went on to tell everyone how much of a gentlemen Zeus was to bring them wine and music. They were all laughing so hard in the Jacuzzi pool that Zeus really didn't have much time to look at their bodies in the water. Little did they know, that Zeus took much notice of both of their bodies when they were in the water and even more notice when Shellie and Hailey got out of the pool. Yes indeed, he watched quite intently as they stooped down to pick up the terry-cloth robes to wrap around their very firm feminine bodies.

Monique finally left her cabin around eleven that morning, having awakened around ten. She had no intention of trying to track Sidney down nor did she want to explain to Joy and company where she was and what she did with Sidney last night. She figured she could avoid the drama if she just slept in late. She was right.

Later that afternoon...

Sidney had gotten through all three of his workout classes with minimal teasing from his coworkers. Most of them merely puckered up their lips whenever they walked past him on deck. Others made a kissing sound if they saw him and then howled with laughter right in his face. There was nothing to explain. The joke was on him and it would die on its own, which wasn't going to be any time too soon. Sidney had learned a valuable lesson about leading an old horse to the water and then kicking it to the curb. *Don't do it.* The payback could be swift and grand. He had pissed off the wrong person. Janeen had feelings that Sidney had tossed to the wind. He deserved what she had done to him. He was lucky she hadn't done more. He owed her an apology, but it would probably be suicidal to try to contact her.

Sidney walked a few feet over to Emerald Palace Lounge to get some sympathy from Howard. Howard looked up and just shook his head.

"I heard about the lipstick on your cabin door, Sid," Howard said sincerely.

"Everyone else has obviously seen and heard about it too. If one more person throws me a kiss, I think I'm gonna be sick."

As the two continued talking, Howard told him about his Jacuzzi adventure with Shellie and Hailey. He particularly mentioned how easy it was to drop his trunks and bare all, giving them a chance to get a good stare at his naked body before he climbed into the pool. Howard was slightly aroused just thinking about it again. Then he told Sidney how tight their bodies were and how lucky he was to get the opportunity to see Hailey's private parts *"one mo time."* Shellie had tried to slip into her robe real fast, but Howard said he sneaked a long peak at her stuff too. Front and back. In fact, he was staring at their bodies while they were in the pool. The two women looked even better outside under the moonlight early this morning. He would never forget the experience.

The two men gave each other a rather loud high five. Sidney was proud of his boy. He had handled things as smoothly as a baby's bottom. He was almost ready for the big league...to hang with the pros. However, Sidney didn't feel like one of the pros now. That little stunt Janeen played on him really busted his balls.

The Farewell Dinner...

It was the ship's last night at sea and also the Captain's Farewell Dinner! Most of the passengers entered the doors to the Garden of Eden fully clad in gowns and tuxedos, and adorned in shiny silver and gold. Shoes were polished and spit shined. The group of five women and two men looked exceptionally stunning in their formal attire. The dinner was a three-course meal with a selection of three entrees, followed by an assortment of desserts, coffee and tea, and champagne. The chef prepared each entree in a beautiful design; and, when their plates arrived they all marveled at the incredible arrangement of delectable foods. They almost hated to disturb their plates because they were so creatively presented.

Serenades the Seas continued its steady voyage to New Orleans throughout the night. Docking time was eight o'clock Sunday morning. The seven-day cruise was coming to an end.

nineteen
farewell

Sunday morning...

The ship docked at
the pier in New Orleans right on time...eight o'clock. A group
of about a hundred people were on land waving and screaming as the ship sounded its arrival horn. The eight went to the
OZ Club Saturday night after the midnight buffet to get in
some serious *last night at sea* partying. Sidney was able to
join them as well. They stopped by the Emerald Palace first to
give farewell hugs and handshakes to Zeus. He was trying to
mix drinks and talk to everyone at the same time. It was a
busy night for him too. Hailey somehow got behind the bar
and gave Zeus a very tight hug and kiss on the cheek. She
wanted to privately thank him for all the laughs, serious talks,
and for their one night together. The others ignored her and
just turned around and continued to talk among themselves.

She winked at Zeus as she walked away to leave. He understood why.

Hailey Woods was ready to say farewell to her image as a party girl, a flirt, an aggressive charmer, needy for attention. Yeah, "Hailey's Den: Lions Welcome" was cute but no longer appropriate for her. She didn't feel bad about what had happened between her and Zeus. He was her friend. She knew it was wrong, but she also knew she would never do *that* again with another person. She wasn't going to be fake and phoney about being a wife. She had learned a lot from Zeus about how she could be perceived by others in a positive way if she herself felt positive about who she was *and* what she did. True, Hailey was attractive and sexy. Also true was the fact that Hailey now knew that with these attributes she could still be looked upon as a lady. Hailey was happy to say farewell to her old unimpressive image and *HEL-LO* to being a beautiful, smart empowered woman who commanded much-deserved respect and admiration from both men and women.

Ms. *Pendulum of Emotions*, Shellie Jackson, was happy to give some serious thought to the possibility of actually saying farewell to a marriage that she worked so hard *solo* to keep. She realized that allowing her life to revolve around her husband's and children's lives had always been a no-win situation for her. Her thinking had changed over the last week while being on this cruise. She now understood how important it was to adjust her priorities and take time out for herself. Her family was going to take from her as long as she did all the giving. It wasn't going to be a big struggle because Shellie wasn't second guessing her instincts if she felt like not doing for her family. She was prepared to use the "No" word.

Shellie was happy to say farewell to those familiar feelings of guilt and to say hello to and embrace her free spirit, her freed mind, and her new feelings of control over her destiny.

Monique Payne was in control of who she was and to what extent she developed emotional feelings toward others, especially men. She felt confident that she could have male friends who could be just that...*male friends*. She was now very conscious of when she began to fall for someone—too soon, too fast, and too hard wasn't happening to her anymore. She simply wasn't going there. If she met a man who had an affect on her, and she on him, she was more than willing to discuss the situation maturely and openly without any of the game playing. If he couldn't, then she wasn't going to waste her time talking to hear herself talk. She was going to start respecting the fact that she had a husband at home and any brotha she met was going to have to respect it as well. She wasn't entertaining any hidden agendas. She had her own agenda and she wasn't going to stray from it. Sidney was a friend; and he was going to stay on his side of the line, or he was out of her life for good. She knew she hadn't *completely* mastered staying on her side yet, but at least she had some limitations. Some didn't. So Monique could honestly say farewell to dealing with all those *lion and tiger and bear men* who are players out for themselves, and hello to honest self-assured men and friendships with them that could enrich her *personally* in some capacity and, at the same time, shed some light on how men and women can interact in a more positive and productive way.

LaNae Nelson...well...she felt good about having Solomon as a loving friend, *not guilty*. Maybe one day Solomon could say hello to Freddy...on second thought... maybe not. LaNae would have to pray on that one. At any rate, she was comfortable about the feelings she had for Solomon. She trusted him not to take advantage of their friendship and cross the line again. She felt blessed to have him in her life as another person who truly loved her, not as a wife, not as a lover, but as a friend. It was possible. Now LaNae knew she was predisposed to taking a giant leap with Solomon if things didn't work out with her husband, but she didn't want Solomon. She had a husband whom she loved very much. She could never want Solomon as her husband because she knew he had issues and would never leave the security of his wife. Men aren't willing to risk it all like women, probably because they know women *are more likely to do the honors*. And so LaNae, content with Solomon, her friend in spirit, would continue to work toward the day that she could honestly say farewell to all temptations to go astray with him.

Last, but not least, was Joy Sharpe, who with baby on the way had much to say farewell and hello to. She not only had to say farewell to a life that used to totally revolve around her, but to a habit of being the busybody in everyone's life and, to not allowing Peter to relieve her of some of the worry she undoubtedly placed on herself. Peter handled things so much better than Joy. He looked at things from a different perspective and without overreacting like she tended to do.

Yes, Joy was going to have to realize that she didn't have all the answers, wasn't the perfectionist she thought she was, and that she could no longer go around controlling other people's lives. Frankly, as a new mother-to-be, she simply wasn't going to have the time. The Girls would now have their chance for payback. It was going to be interesting to see how receptive Joy was to what they had to say about raising a child. And so Joy could say *Hey!* to the upcoming experience of giving birth; to watching her child grow up to become a compassionate, intelligent, and responsible loving adult; and to sharing her life with Peter with another person.

After the ship docked, the seven, minus Sidney who was sailing again in three days, had about three hours to walk the brick pavements of the French Quarter before getting to the airport for their mid-afternoon flights back to Cincinnati, Ohio, and then on to their home states of Indiana and Maryland. As always, the streets of New Orleans had enough scenery and music for both tourists and city inhabitants to enjoy immensely.

As they walked to their gate in the New Orleans airport, the cruise would most certainly be remembered by each of the women and for different reasons—mainly because of the *lions and tigers and bears* who had an impact on their lives that week. Joy and her girls had cruised together on *Serenades the Seas*, and Joy's personal dream of them being together in Oz had been brought to life. The yellow brick road was behind them...

"...*Just sit back, relax, and enjoy the ride...Once again...welcome aboard our nonstop flight to Cincinnati...*" the Captain of the flight said about three minutes after their plane was in the air.

The End

About Alicia!

Lions & Tigers & Bears is the third book written by author Alicia Williams (pen name). It is a sequel to her first adult fiction book titled, *The Scarecrow, The Lion & The Tinman: A Novelette About Forbidden Friendships* (1996, softcover). Alicia's second book was a nonfiction book titled, *Women Behind The Men Behind The Badge: Their Stories* (1997, paperback). Both books were published by Écrivez!, her Columbus, Ohio-based small press company. She is now working on her fourth book, a nonfiction paperback, to be available in the year 2000.

Currently residing in Columbus, Ohio, Alicia attended The Ohio State University where she earned her B.A. degree in Journalism and M.A. in Communications. She has over 18 years of work experience as a technical writer/editor. She is also sole proprietor of Écrivez! The WRITE Look, her writing and consulting firm.

Alicia is an experienced speaker and workshop leader. She delivers presentations at professional conferences and community events. Her three workshops are titled, "Writing With a Passion to Publish," "Talk To The Badge: Maintaining Healthy Communications," and "Women Behind Men Wearing A Badge."

As a featured author on the "Not for Writers Only" television show, Alicia was interviewed on topics such as fiction/nonfiction writing, self-publishing, marketing and selling books, and operating and owning your own business.